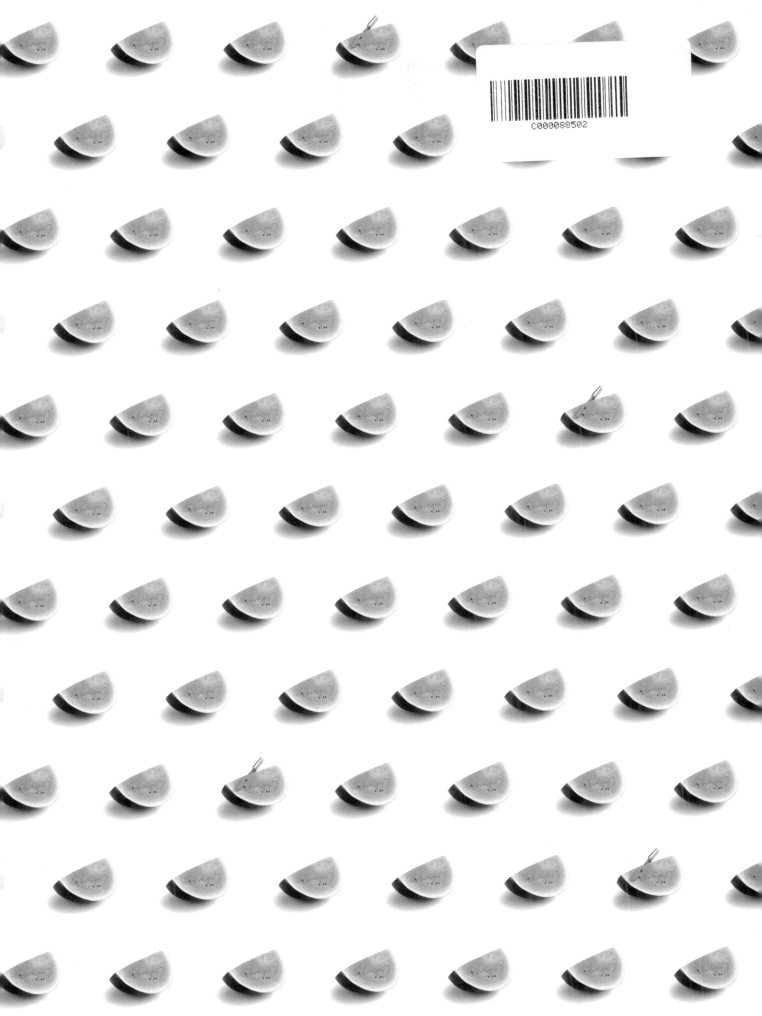

KiDS'
cooking for health

THE AUSTRALIAN

Women's Weekly

KiDS'
cooking for health

easy recipes that teach kids to cook

acp
books

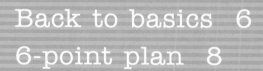C•ntents

Denotes that kids eight years and older can, under adult supervision, try cooking these recipes for themselves.

Back to basics

Relax. Kids' health can be good fun for everyone and it doesn't need to be all doom and gloom. Seven million Australian adults (54% of the adult population) were classified as obese in 2004-05, but your children need not be a part of this statistic. Get back to basics and foster a healthy family attitude to wellbeing and you're halfway there.

The goal is to achieve a balance between the lifestyle factors we can't avoid and the positive things we can do.

Lifestyle factors we can't avoid include television, computers and video games, as well as those fantastic marketing campaigns by the producers of unhealthy foods.

There is no doubt about it, "screen time" is here to stay. On average, children spend about 2 hours every weekday watching television, videos or DVDs and also spend an additional hour playing electronic or computer games. By comparison, only 63% of children aged 5-14 years participate in sport outside of school hours. Keep a record of how much screen time versus exercise time your child engages in – you will probably be shocked at the results. But there is no need for alarm. This is now, like it or not, the usual case. It is simply time to adapt by embracing better eating habits to offset all those sedentary lifestyle patterns that are now a routine way of life.

A crucial part of the battle starts at home. Studies show that children begin to develop their attitude to food as early as two years of age. Learning to have a relaxed, self-regulated, healthy approach to food is a skill they will be grateful for their whole life.

This is where getting back to basics comes in.

Encouraging them to listen to their tummies, eat a variety of food types and understand food and nutrition while limiting their exposure to "unhealthy foods" are important and relatively easy ways to teach this skill.

Common concerns from parents about kids' diets include too little or too large an appetite; pickiness about food types; and the question of how to achieve a balanced diet in a world of targeted advertising and sedentary lifestyle arrangements.

With the help of the recipes in this book, and the following six point plan, your kids will be on their way to better health.

6-point plan

1. Quality of diet

In a perfect world, it would be ideal to have these five groups included in your child's diet. **Protein** is needed for strong and healthy bodies. Dairy products such as yogurt, milk and cheese are perfect, as is white and red lean meat, fish and dried beans and peas. **Vegetables and fruit** for nutrients and fibre. Variety is the key with fruit and vegies so build a rainbow of colours in meals for kids. Even get them to sing along to *I Can Sing a Rainbow* and include vegetables that are red and yellow, pink, green, orange, purple and blue. Well, maybe not blue, but including a wide spectrum of colours maximises nutrients and protective components in their diet. As a lot of the fibre and nutrients in fruit and vegetables sit directly under the skin, make the most of them and keep their skin on. **Starchy carbohydrates** are the energy blocks that keep kids powering through the day. The higher the fibre content, the more slowly the energy will burn off – keeping kids focused and active throughout the day. Choose fibre-enriched bread instead of plain white bread, wholegrain foods, basmati rice, and wheat foods such as pasta.

Friendly fats are necessary every day, within reason. Fat provides energy, helps to make the hormone-like compounds that regulate body processes and also builds brain and nerve cells. Monounsaturated and polyunsaturated fats both tend to lower blood cholesterol when they replace saturated fats in the diet, with the latter being more effective. Include a little of the friendly fats every day and keep saturated fats to a minimum.

- **Polyunsaturated fats:** vegetable oils, margarines.
- **Monounsaturated fats:** olive and canola oils, avocado.
- **Omega-3 (polyunsaturated) fats:** fish oils found in deep sea fish such as salmon and tuna, walnuts and linseeds.
- **Omega-6 (polyunsaturated) fats:** nuts, seeds and their oils.

Tap water is the cheapest and best way to fix a thirst. An essential part of any diet, it also contains fluoride for strong teeth. Don't forget that juice, even freshly squeezed juice, can simply fill kids up without a great deal of nutritional benefit. If you want to give kids juice, mix it half and half with water.

What your kids should eat everyday

The Dietary Guidelines for Children and Adolescents in Australia suggests the following daily intake. Keep a record of what your child eats for a day, and compare this with the suggested amounts below.

Food Groups	Children 4-7 years	Children 8-11 years	Adolescents 12-18 years	Sample serving
Cereals (bread, rice, pasta, noodles)	5-7 servings	6-9 servings	5-11 servings	2 slices of bread; 1 medium bread roll; 1 cup cooked rice, pasta or noodles; 1 cup porridge; 1⅓ cups breakfast cereal; ½ cup muesli
Vegetables, legumes	2-4 servings	3-5 servings	4-9 servings	1 medium potato; ½ cup dark green leafy vegetables; ½ cup cooked vegetables, dried peas, beans or lentils; 1 cup salad vegetables
Fruit	1-2 servings	1-2 servings	3-4 servings	1 medium piece (apple, banana, orange); 2 small pieces (apricot, kiwifruit, plum); ½ cup fruit juice; 4 dried apricots; 1 cup canned fruit
Milk, yogurt, cheese	2 servings	2 servings	3 servings	1 cup milk; ½ cup evaporated milk; 2 slices cheese; ¾ cup yogurt; 1 cup custard; 1 cup almonds
Lean meat, fish, poultry, eggs, nuts, legumes	½ serving	1 serving	1 serving	65-100g cooked meat or chicken; ½ cup cooked beans or lentils; 1 small fish fillet; 3 fish fingers; a small can of tuna or salmon; 2 small eggs; ⅓ cup peanuts or almonds

Tip **Milk** Get kids to drink their milk by making smoothies or milkshakes – often a more appealing option than just plain milk. After 2 years of age, children don't need to drink full-cream milk – low-fat milk or 1½% fat milk is perfect. Children under 5 years old should not have skim milk (99.9% fat free).

2.
Appetite Control

Latest research shows that the best practice when it comes to swinging appetites is to trust your child's tummy to get the balance right. Fluctuations in levels of activity and rate of growth mean children's appetites change all the time. At about age two, children suddenly need much less food, and this can be a danger time for developing poor eating habits. Parents try to make children eat more than they actually need, bribe them, or provide unhealthy food in an attempt to get them to eat.

Tips **Division of responsibility** You decide what to offer children and they decide how much to eat. This teaches healthy eating habits, and allows you to control what is offered. Making children responsible for their food intake teaches healthy eating habits and helps them understand about food and nutrition.

New foods Children may not even taste a new type of food until it is offered to them 6-10 times. When introducing something new, put a small amount on their plate several times over – they will eventually try it. It helps if they see you eating it, but if you have trouble, stop, and try again in 3-6 months.

If you think they are not eating enough, remember that, as long as they are gaining weight and are active and healthy, they are likely getting enough kilojoules. Forcing children with a small appetite to eat when they aren't hungry teaches poor eating habits; they need to learn how to regulate their own intake by responding to how full they feel. Obviously, sweets, chips and biscuits can suppress their appetite for nutritious food. Not so obviously, milk and fruit juices can also fill them up.

If your youngster's appetite seems too big, try to slow the eating process down. Offer portions of foods with the most nutrition first – lean protein and vegetables. When they've eaten these, offer a normal portion of starchy carbohydrates.

It can take up to 20 minutes after eating for the brain to get the message that your stomach is full. So, offer half the meal, wait 10 minutes then offer the second half, once their brain catches up to their tummies.

3.
Exercise

Physical activity for kids is as crucially important as a healthy diet. It is the second wave of ammunition in the battle against unavoidable unhealthy lifestyle factors. Exercise is vital in children between 2 and 12 years of age for healthy growth and development. It is a way to make friends, and can help establish a health routine that will stay with them their whole lives. The Australian Government provides the following guidelines for physical activity: Children need a minimum of 60 minutes of moderate to vigorous physical activity every day.

Children should not spend more than two hours a day using electronic media for entertainment, particularly during daylight hours.

Involve children in extra-curricular activities such as swimming or team sports, and encourage them to play outside during the day rather than spending time indoors. Limit the time they are allowed to spend on sedentary entertainment.

As a parent or carer, don't take your position as a role model lightly. If children see you participate in a range of physical activity, they will be encouraged to follow your lead.

4.
Family values

Sitting around the dinner table with all family members present seems like something out of a Hollywood movie. With both parents working and children engaged in all sorts of before and after-school activity, fleeting and fractured visits to the dining table does seem unavoidable.

At an age where children are like sponges – soaking everything up to form opinions and behaviours – family meals are actually an important part of getting children to eat healthily, and to have a healthy relationship with food. Table manners, social skills, and an interest in home-cooked food all come from observing their role models (that's you) in action.

Although they want to throw food, use their fingers to eat and interrupt the conversation, by sitting with older family members they will work out what is acceptable and normal behaviour. Seeing siblings and parents enjoy a wide variety of food, accompaniments and

drinks will encourage them to be more adventurous and interested in food.

Parents can make meal times a fun and educational experience by following a few simple guidelines:

- **Turn off the television.**
- **Mind your own manners.**
- **Attempt to have the meal at the same time each night.**
- **Expect family to spend a reasonable amount of time at the table.**
- **Make the meal time a relaxing event.**
- **Change the scenery – perhaps take a picnic to the park, or even just the backyard for something a bit different.**
- **Talk about where the food you are eating has come from.**

If you can, it's also a great idea to schedule in a meal out at least once a week. Not only does it give you a night off from preparing and cooking a meal, but your children's tastebuds will be exposed to the amazing world of food. Naturally, takeaway food is not ideal too often, so stick to the fabulous family-friendly recipes in this book the rest of the time.

Did you know?

Takeaway foods that appear to be healthy can sometimes be loaded with fat, salt and sugar. Ask if a nutrition leaflet is available – you may find that it's not as healthy as you think.

5.
Smart snacking & sometime foods

With little tummies and big energy needs, kids need regular in-between meal snacks. Snacks are a minefield of brightly-coloured sugary, fat-filled and low-energy foods marketed by super-powered cartoon characters. So it's no wonder they have been partially blamed for the "obesity epidemic".

The right snacks, however, really can super-power your kids by boosting energy and concentration at school, and can help meet nutrient requirements. Play the game with the same tricks the big snack-food companies play and at least you'll be in with a chance. By presenting food in a fun way and employing basic marketing skills in your house you'll be able to get them to eat just about anything.

Marketing at home starts with the presentation. A very attractive part of pre-packaged snacks is that they tend to be very simple to prepare (or require no preparation), single serving items. Adopt this strategy with your healthy snacks, too. Cut fruit is much more appealing to kids than whole fruit, so tempt them with a plate of brightly coloured pre-cut fruit. Mini muffins are tempting, too, and can be made that little bit more special by warming for 10 seconds in the microwave.

It can be difficult avoiding constant requests for "not-so-smart" snacks. Identify times your children tend to snack and be prepared – hungry children will eat whatever is available. Is the sound of a dumped school bag followed by the sound of an opening fridge or cupboard door familiar? After school is a very common snack time so be ready. Instead of having chocolate or muesli bars in the fridge, have ready-cut carrots or celery, soup and yogurt. In the cupboard, keep dried fruit and nuts or snack-sized cans of baked beans at eye-level where the kids can see them, and keep treats where they can't be seen.

The other important message to get through to kids is the concept of "sometime foods". Talk to your children in terms of "everyday" and "sometime" foods, rather than good and bad foods. There is a place for all food in a healthy diet – frequency and quantity are the things to watch out for.

Restricting some foods completely can lead to "forbidden fruit syndrome", where children gorge themselves on the very food they have been told to avoid. This can cause uninhibited eating and may lead to weight gain, particularly in girls.

Decide on treat times together; if kids feel you are making a compromise, they are more willing to compromise, too. Don't budge once you've come to your agreement. Treat time might be on the way home from a particular sport practice or a once-a-week order from the school canteen – whatever the arrangement, consistency is the key.

 Did you know?

Not all sports and energy drinks are the right thing for children to be drinking. Energy drinks usually have very high levels of caffeine, so kids should drink them with caution. Sports drinks can have excellent benefits for children involved in competition sport, but may be an unnecessary sugar hit for those who are drinking them purely for the taste.

Fun factor

If food is bland, and meal-times boring, it is no wonder kids are attracted to catchy commercial jingles and super-heroes on packages. But spice things up and make food interesting, and you'll soon get their attention.

Get kids to help out in the kitchen. Meal preparation can help kids learn so much about food and nutrition. It can seem like quite a task to allow little hands into the kitchen, but if you relax a bit about cleanliness, choose a good time to do it (like a Sunday morning), and stick to our kid-friendly recipes, you and the kids will have a ball.

Make the most of the opportunity and emphasise the benefits of clean hands, keeping hair out of food, and tidying up as you go. It's also a good time to teach them about handling raw meat and what kitchen utensils they can and can't use.

Before you start, read through the ingredient list and method with them and talk about the equipment you'll need. Get kids started using plastic knives and stirring the mixture before they move onto real knives and cooking over heat.

1.

A good breakfast

✳ Corn, cheese and carrot omelettes

ingredients

8 eggs
310g can creamed corn
1 large carrot (180g), grated coarsely
¼ cup finely chopped fresh flat-leaf parsley
½ cup (60g) coarsely grated reduced-fat
    cheddar cheese

A quick and easy before-school tummy-filler. Add a slice of crisp bacon or even a few pan-fried mushrooms to the omelette, if you like.

method

1 Whisk eggs in medium bowl until combined; stir in remaining ingredients.
2 Pour a quarter of the egg mixture into heated oiled small frying pan; cook over medium heat until omelette is set. Fold omelette in half, slide onto plate; cover to keep warm.
3 Repeat process with remaining egg mixture to make four omelettes.

preparation time *10 minutes* cooking time *20 minutes* serves *4* nutritional count per serving *14.7g total fat (5.6g saturated fat); 1162kJ (278 cal); 15.3g carbohydrate; 19.6g protein; 4g fibre*

1. Buttermilk fruit smoothie

Blend or process 1 small coarsely chopped pear, 1 small coarsely chopped banana, 2 teaspoons honey, ½ cup buttermilk and ½ cup apple juice until smooth. Pour into glass; serve with ice.

preparation time *5 minutes* serves *1* nutritional count per serving *2.8g total fat (1.7g saturated fat); 1488kJ (356 cal); 71.2g carbohydrate; 7.5g protein; 6g fibre*

Freeze unpeeled bananas then use them straight from the freezer to give your smoothie an ice-creamy texture.

2. Strawberry smoothie

Soften 200g low-fat frozen strawberry yogurt slightly; cut into pieces. Hull 250g strawberries; cut each in half. Blend or process yogurt, strawberries and 1 litre low-fat milk, in batches, until smooth.

preparation time *10 minutes* serves *4* nutritional count per serving *0.7g total fat (0.3g saturated fat); 723kJ (173 cal); 25g carbohydrate; 15.6g protein; 1.4g fibre*

3. Banana smoothie

Blend or process 2 cups skim milk, 2 coarsely chopped medium bananas, ½ cup low-fat yogurt, 1 tablespoon honey, 1 tablespoon wheat germ and ¼ teaspoon ground cinnamon until smooth.

preparation time *5 minutes* serves *4* nutritional count per serving *0.4g total fat (0.2g saturated fat); 648kJ (155 cal); 28.3g carbohydrate; 8.3g protein; 1.8g fibre*

Use frozen bananas or add ice cubes to blender for a thicker smoothie.

4. Pear smoothie

Blend or process 2 medium coarsely chopped pears, 2 cups soy milk and 1 tablespoon honey until smooth.

preparation time *5 minutes* serves *4* nutritional count per serving *2.8g total fat (0g saturated fat); 589kJ (141 cal); 25.5g carbohydrate; 1.9g protein; 2.6g fibre*

1

3

2

4

✳ Baked eggs with ham and cheese

ingredients

50g shaved ham, chopped coarsely
2 green onions, chopped finely
4 eggs
⅓ cup (40g) coarsely grated cheddar cheese

method

1 Preheat oven to 180°C/160°C fan-forced. Oil four ½-cup (125ml) ovenproof dishes.
2 Divide ham and onion among dishes. Break one egg into small bowl; carefully slide egg over ham and onion in dish. Repeat with remaining eggs. Sprinkle dishes with equal amounts of cheese.
3 Place dishes on oven tray; bake about 10 minutes or until egg is just set.

preparation time *10 minutes* cooking time *10 minutes* serves *4* nutritional count per serving *9.1g total fat (3.9g saturated fat); 539kJ (129 cal); 0.4g carbohydrate; 11.6g protein; 0.1g fibre*

By breaking the eggs into a small bowl first, you will be able to discard any bad eggs without ruining the other ingredients in the dish; also, by sliding the egg carefully into the dish it's less likely to splash.

23

ingredients

4 eggs, beaten lightly
6 egg whites
500g swiss brown mushrooms, sliced thinly
⅓ cup loosely packed, coarsely chopped
    fresh flat-leaf parsley

method

1 Whisk beaten egg with egg white in medium bowl.
2 Cook mushrooms in heated oiled 20cm frying pan, stirring, until tender. Combine mushrooms and parsley in small bowl.
3 Return pan to heat, add a quarter of the egg mixture; cook, tilting pan, over medium heat until almost set. Place a quarter of the mushroom mixture evenly over half of the omelette; fold omelette over to enclose filling, slide onto serving plate. Repeat with remaining egg and mushroom mixture to make four omelettes in total.
4 Serve omelettes with thick slices of toasted sourdough, if you like.

preparation time 10 minutes cooking time 10 minutes serves 4 nutritional count per serving 5.6g total fat (1.6g saturated fat); 531kJ (127 cal); 0.7g carbohydrate; 16.6g protein; 3.4g fibre

cook's info
Basil can be substituted for the parsley, if you like.

*Mushroom and parsley omelette

Egg-white omelette

ingredients

12 egg whites
4 green onions, chopped finely
¼ cup finely chopped fresh chives
¼ cup finely chopped fresh chervil
½ cup finely chopped fresh flat-leaf parsley
½ cup (60g) coarsely grated cheddar cheese
½ cup (50g) coarsely grated mozzarella cheese

method

1 Beat a quarter of the egg white in small bowl with electric mixer until soft peaks form; fold in a quarter of the combined onion and herbs.
2 Pour mixture into heated oiled 20cm frying pan; cook, uncovered, over low heat until omelette is just browned lightly on the bottom.
3 Preheat grill.
4 Sprinkle a quarter of the combined cheeses over half the omelette. Place pan under grill until cheese begins to melt and omelette sets; fold omelette over to completely cover cheese. Carefully slide onto serving plate; cover to keep warm.
5 Repeat process three times with remaining egg white, onion and herb mixture, and cheese. Serve with roast tomatoes and toast, if you like.

preparation time *25 minutes* cooking time *20 minutes* serves *4* nutritional count per serving *7.9g total fat (5g saturated fat); 620kJ (148 cal); 1.1g carbohydrate; 18.2g protein; 0.7g fibre*

Apple and raisin french toast

ingredients

1 large apple (200g)
2 tablespoons water
¼ cup (40g) coarsely chopped raisins
½ loaf unsliced white bread (320g)
3 eggs
½ cup (125ml) low-fat milk
1 tablespoon honey
½ teaspoon finely grated orange rind
½ teaspoon ground cinnamon
20g butter
2 tablespoons icing sugar

method

1 Peel, core then thinly slice apple.
2 Place apple and the water in small saucepan; bring to the boil. Reduce heat; simmer, covered, about 5 minutes or until apple is just tender. Remove from heat; stir in raisins. Cool 15 minutes.
3 Meanwhile, slice bread into quarters; cut each piece three-quarters of the way through. Divide apple mixture among bread pockets.
4 Whisk eggs in medium bowl; whisk in milk, honey, rind and cinnamon.
5 Heat half the butter in large frying pan. Dip two bread pockets into egg mixture, one at a time; cook, uncovered, until browned both sides.
6 Remove from pan; cover to keep warm. Repeat with remaining butter and bread. Cut pockets into quarters; serve sprinkled with sifted icing sugar.

preparation time *20 minutes (plus cooling time)*
cooking time *15 minutes* serves *4*
nutritional count per serving
10.3g total fat (4.3g saturated fat); 1668kJ (399 cal); 60.6g carbohydrate; 13.6g protein; 3.5g fibre

✳ Pancetta and eggs

ingredients

8 slices pancetta (120g)
2 green onions, chopped coarsely
4 eggs
4 thick slices white bread

method

1 Preheat oven to 200°C/180°C fan-forced. Oil four holes of 12-hole (⅓-cup/80ml) muffin pan.
2 Line each hole with 2 slices of pancetta, overlapping to form cup shape. Divide onion among pancetta cups; break one egg into each pancetta cup.
3 Bake, uncovered, about 10 minutes or until eggs are just cooked and pancetta is crisp around the edges. Remove from pan carefully.
4 Meanwhile, toast bread until browned lightly both sides. Serve pancetta and eggs on toast.

preparation time *5 minutes* cooking time *10 minutes* serves *4* nutritional count per serving *10.1g total fat (3.3g saturated fat); 853kJ (204 cal); 13.1g carbohydrate; 14.9g protein; 0.9g fibre*

ingredients

600g spinach, trimmed, chopped coarsely
4 rashers rindless bacon (250g)
4 eggs
⅓ cup (25g) pecorino cheese flakes

method

1 Boil, steam or microwave spinach until just wilted; drain. Cover to keep warm.
2 Heat large frying pan; cook bacon until crisp. Drain on absorbent paper; cover to keep warm.
3 Half-fill the same pan with water; bring to the boil. Break one egg into small bowl; slide into pan. Repeat with remaining eggs; when all eggs are in pan, allow water to return to the boil. Cover pan, turn off heat; stand about 4 minutes or until a light film of egg white sets over yolks. Using an egg slide, remove eggs one at a time from pan; place on absorbent-paper-lined saucer to blot up poaching liquid.
4 Divide spinach among serving plates; top with bacon, egg then cheese.

preparation time 5 minutes cooking time 10 minutes
serves 4 nutritional count per serving 16.6g total fat
(3.9g saturated fat); 828kJ (198 cal); 0.9g carbohydrate;
23.6g protein; 2.1g fibre

✳ Poached eggs with bacon, spinach and pecorino

1. Orange, mango and strawberry juice

Juice 2 small oranges on citrus squeezer; pour into glass. Blend or process 1 small coarsely chopped mango and 3 hulled strawberries until smooth; stir into orange juice.

preparation time *5 minutes* serves *1*
nutritional count per serving *0.7g total fat (0g saturated fat); 949kJ (227 cal); 48.7g carbohydrate; 5.7g protein; 9.6g fibre*

2. Raspberry and peach juice

Blend or process 1 large coarsely chopped peach and ¼ cup raspberries until smooth; pour into glass. Stir in ½ cup water.

preparation time *5 minutes* serves *1*
nutritional count per serving *0.3g total fat (0g saturated fat); 301kJ (72 cal); 14.1g carbohydrate; 2.1g protein; 4.5g fibre*

3. Orange, carrot and celery juice

Peel and quarter 1 large orange. Coarsely chop 1 large carrot and 1 trimmed celery stalk. Push ingredients through juice extractor into glass; stir to combine.

preparation time *5 minutes* serves *1*
nutritional count per serving *0.5g total fat (0g saturated fat); 573kJ (137 cal); 28.6g carbohydrate; 4.2g protein; 11.3g fibre*

4. Apple and pear juice

Cut 1 medium apple and 1 medium pear into wedges. Push fruit through juice extractor into glass; stir to combine.

preparation time *5 minutes* serves *1*
nutritional count per serving *0.4g total fat (0g saturated fat); 853kJ (204 cal); 51.3g carbohydrate; 1.1g protein; 9g fibre*

We used a green apple in this recipe, but you can use whatever type you like.

Top Tip

Breakfast is the most important meal of the day. It is the fuel that gives your body the energy that is necessary for good health, and keeps kids alert in school.

ingredients

2 teaspoons olive oil
1 tablespoon pine nuts
2 cloves garlic, crushed
100g baby spinach leaves
1¼ cups (300g) low-fat ricotta cheese
1 egg, beaten lightly
2 tablespoons coarsely chopped fresh chives
500g baby vine-ripened truss tomatoes
1 tablespoon balsamic vinegar

method

1 Preheat oven to 220°C/200°C fan-forced. Oil four holes of a 6-hole (⅓-cup/80ml) muffin pan.
2 Heat half the oil in medium frying pan; cook pine nuts and garlic until fragrant. Add spinach; stir until wilted. Cool 10 minutes.
3 Combine spinach mixture in medium bowl with cheese, egg and chives; divide among pan holes. Bake about 15 minutes or until browned.
4 Combine tomatoes and vinegar with remaining oil in small shallow baking dish. Roast, uncovered, 10 minutes.
5 Serve baked ricotta with tomatoes.
preparation time *15 minutes* cooking time *20 minutes* serves *4* nutritional count per serving *12.9g total fat (5.1g saturated fat); 777kJ (186 cal); 4.7g carbohydrate; 11.9g protein; 2.7g fibre*

Baked ricotta with tomato

* Cheesy scrambled eggs with spinach

ingredients

8 eggs
⅓ cup (80g) reduced-fat spreadable cream cheese
50g baby spinach leaves, chopped coarsely

method

1 Whisk eggs in medium bowl until combined. Whisk in cheese and spinach.
2 Cook mixture, stirring gently, in heated oiled medium frying pan over low heat until almost set. Serve with wholemeal toast, if you like.

preparation time 5 minutes cooking time 5 minutes serves 4 nutritional count per serving 13.8g total fat (5.4g saturated fat); 790kJ (189 cal); 1g carbohydrate; 15.3g protein; 0.3g fibre

Light-white frittata

ingredients

½ cup (80g) fresh shelled peas
1 medium yellow capsicum (200g), sliced thinly
1 small kumara (250g), grated coarsely
12 egg whites
½ cup (120g) light sour cream
1 cup loosely packed fresh basil leaves
¼ cup (20g) finely grated parmesan cheese

method

1 Cook peas, capsicum and kumara in heated oiled 20cm frying pan, stirring, until just tender.
2 Meanwhile, whisk egg whites and sour cream in medium bowl; stir in basil.
3 Pour egg-white mixture over vegetables; cook, covered, over low heat about 10 minutes or until frittata is almost set.
4 Meanwhile, preheat grill.
5 Sprinkle cheese over frittata; place under grill until frittata is set and top is browned lightly.
   preparation time *15 minutes* cooking time *20 minutes* serves *4* nutritional count per serving *7.8g total fat (4.9g saturated fat); 815kJ (195 cal); 13g carbohydrate; 16.7g protein; 2.8g fibre*

You need to buy 200g of fresh peas in their pods to get the amount of shelled peas required for this recipe. You can use frozen peas instead of fresh peas, if you like.

Frittata can be served hot or at room temperature.

Freeze leftover egg yolks, in small containers of two or four, for future use when baking or when making custard.

✳Baked beans, bacon and tomato on toast

ingredients

2 medium tomatoes (300g), chopped coarsely
1 tablespoon finely chopped chives
420g can baked beans in tomato sauce
4 rindless bacon rashers (250g), chopped coarsely
½ large loaf turkish bread (215g), halved

method

1 Preheat grill.
2 Combine tomato and chives in small bowl.
3 Heat beans in small saucepan.
4 Meanwhile, cook bacon in heated small frying pan, stirring, until crisp; drain on absorbent paper.
5 Cut bread pieces horizontally; toast cut sides. Top toast with beans, bacon and tomato mixture; grill about 2 minutes or until hot.

preparation time *5 minutes* cooking time *5 minutes* serves *4* nutritional count per serving *10.4g total fat (3.2g saturated fat); 1450kJ (347 cal); 37.5g carbohydrate; 22g protein; 7.4g fibre*

ingredients

½ loaf ciabatta bread (220g)
200g low-fat ricotta cheese
2 tablespoons honey
1 teaspoon finely grated orange rind
¼ teaspoon ground cinnamon
125g strawberries, sliced thickly
1 small banana (130g), sliced thinly
2 tablespoons brown sugar

method

1 Preheat grill.
2 Trim ends from bread; cut into eight slices.
3 Beat cheese, honey, rind and cinnamon in small bowl with electric mixer until smooth.
4 Combine strawberry, banana and sugar in small frying pan; stir gently over low heat until sugar dissolves.
5 Toast bread both sides. Spread with cheese mixture, divide among plates; top with strawberry mixture.

preparation time *15 minutes* cooking time *10 minutes* serves *4* nutritional count per serving *5.8g total fat (3g saturated fat); 1208kJ (289 cal); 49g carbohydrate; 10.8g protein; 2.8g fibre*

Bruschetta with strawberry, banana and ricotta

1. Fresh berry frappé

Blend or process 300g blueberries and 250g raspberries until just smooth. Push berry puree through fine sieve into large jug; discard solids in sieve. Stir 40 crushed ice cubes and ½ cup fresh orange juice into puree; pour into serving glasses.

preparation time *10 minutes* serves *4* nutritional count per serving *0.4g total fat (0g saturated fat); 322kJ (77 cal); 14.6g carbohydrate; 1.4g protein; 4.8g fibre*

Depending on the sweetness of the berries, you may need to add sugar.
You can also use frozen berries for this recipe. Experiment with other berries – strawberries, blackberries, boysenberries – and adjust combinations to your taste.

2. Pineapple and mint frappé

The word frappé is a French description for frozen or chilled drinks and dishes.

Blend or process 1 large peeled, coarsely chopped pineapple until smooth; transfer to large jug. Stir in 40 crushed ice cubes and 1 tablespoon finely chopped fresh mint; pour into serving glasses.

preparation time *20 minutes* serves *4* nutritional count per serving *0.3g total fat (0g saturated fat); 451kJ (108 cal); 20.8g carbohydrate; 2.6g protein; 5.5g fibre*

You can crush the ice in a blender or food processor.

3. Tropical fruit lassi

Blend or process 1 cup low-fat yogurt, ½ cup water, 100g seeded, coarsely chopped rockmelon, 100g coarsely chopped peeled pineapple, 1 small coarsely chopped mango, 100g hulled strawberries, 1 tablespoon caster sugar and 6 ice cubes until smooth.

preparation time *15 minutes* serves *4* nutritional count per serving *0.3g total fat (0.1g saturated fat); 447kJ (107 cal); 19.1g carbohydrate; 5.5g protein; 2.1g fibre*

Vary the fruit according to the season and your preferences.
Buy the smallest pineapple and rockmelon you can find for this recipe, as you need only 100g of both – you can eat what's left as part of a fruit salad later.

4. Melonade

Combine ½ cup lemon juice and 2 tablespoons caster sugar in small saucepan; stir over low heat until sugar dissolves. Cool. Blend or process 3 cups coarsely chopped watermelon, in batches, until smooth; strain through sieve into large jug. Stir in lemon syrup and 1½ cups sparkling mineral water; serve immediately.

preparation time *10 minutes (plus cooling time)* serves *4* nutritional count per serving *0.3g total fat (0.8g saturated fat); 301kJ (72 cal); 16.1g carbohydrate; 0.6g protein; 0.8g fibre*

You need a 1kg piece of watermelon for this recipe.

1 3
2 4

Strawberry hotcakes with blueberry sauce

ingredients

1 egg, separated
2 egg whites, extra
½ cup (125ml) apple sauce
1 teaspoon vanilla extract
2 cups (560g) low-fat yogurt
1¾ cups (270g) wholemeal self-raising flour
250g strawberries, hulled, chopped coarsely
blueberry sauce
150g blueberries, chopped coarsely
2 tablespoons white sugar
1 tablespoon water

preparation time *15 minutes*
cooking time *20 minutes* serves *4*
nutritional count per serving
*2.6g total fat (0.7g saturated fat);
1814kJ (434 cal); 78.9g carbohydrate;
19.9g protein; 5.1g fibre*

method

1 Make blueberry sauce.
2 Using electric mixer, beat all egg whites in small bowl until soft peaks form. Combine egg yolk, apple sauce, extract, yogurt, flour and strawberry in large bowl; fold in egg whites.
3 Pour ¼ cup of the batter into heated large greased frying pan; using spatula, spread batter a round shape. Cook, over low heat, about 2 minutes or until bubbles appear on the surface. Turn hotcake; cook until browned lightly on other side. Remove from pan; cover to keep warm. Repeat with remaining batter.
4 Serve hotcakes with blueberry sauce.
   blueberry sauce Place ingredients in small saucepan; bring to the boil, stirring constantly. Reduce heat, simmer 2 minutes. Remove from heat; cool 10 minutes. Blend or process blueberry mixture until smooth.

You need only small quantities of pineapple and rockmelon for this recipe, so buy the smallest ones you can find. Two passionfruit will supply the right amount of pulp.

✳ Fruit salad with honey yogurt

ingredients
¾ cup (210g) low-fat yogurt
2 tablespoons honey
200g coarsely chopped pineapple
200g seeded, coarsely chopped rockmelon
250g strawberries, hulled, halved
250g blueberries
1 large banana (230g), sliced thinly
2 tablespoons passionfruit pulp
2 teaspoons lime juice
12 fresh mint leaves

method
1 Combine yogurt and honey in small bowl.
2 Just before serving, combine remaining ingredients in large bowl; serve with honey yogurt.
preparation time *15 minutes* serves *4*
nutritional count per serving *0.4g total fat
(0g saturated fat); 828kJ (198 cal);
38.3g carbohydrate; 6.4g protein; 6.5g fibre*

Lime juice not only adds flavour to this recipe but also prevents the banana from discolouring.

You need two passionfruit for this recipe.

ingredients

1 cup (240g) low-fat ricotta cheese
¾ cup (210g) low-fat tropical yogurt
2 small mangoes (600g)
2 english muffins
2 tablespoons passionfruit pulp

method

1 Whisk cheese and yogurt together in medium bowl until mixture is smooth.
2 Slice cheeks from mangoes; remove skin, cut each cheek in half.
3 Cook mango on heated oiled grill plate (or grill or barbecue) until browned both sides.
4 Just before serving, split muffins; toast both sides. Place half a muffin on each serving plate; top with cheese mixture and mango, drizzle with passionfruit pulp.
preparation time *10 minutes* cooking time *5 minutes* serves *4* nutritional count per serving *6g total fat (3.5g saturated fat); 1053kJ (252 cal); 33.6g carbohydrate; 13.5g protein; 3.9g fibre*

✳Grilled mango and ricotta with english muffins

You need four trimmed rhubarb stalks for this recipe or, if you like, you can use frozen rhubarb, instead.

ingredients

2 cups (220g) coarsely chopped fresh rhubarb stalks
¼ cup (55g) caster sugar
½ cup (125ml) water
½ teaspoon ground cinnamon
1⅓ cups (375g) low-fat vanilla yogurt
⅓ cup (45g) toasted muesli

method

1 Combine rhubarb, sugar, the water and cinnamon in medium saucepan; bring to the boil. Reduce heat; simmer, uncovered, stirring occasionally, about 10 minutes or until rhubarb is tender. Transfer to medium heatproof bowl, cover; refrigerate 1 hour.
2 Divide rhubarb mixture among four ¾-cup (180ml) serving glasses; top with yogurt then muesli.
preparation time *10 minutes (plus refrigeration time)*
cooking time *10 minutes* serves 4
nutritional count per serving *1.5g total fat (0.5g saturated fat); 782kJ (187 cal); 33.9g carbohydrate; 7.4g protein; 2.9g fibre*

Rhubarb, muesli and yogurt cups

47

ingredients

2 cups (220g) natural muesli
1⅓ cups (330ml) apple juice
¾ cup (210g) low-fat country-style yogurt
1¼ cups (185g) dried peaches, chopped coarsely
2 tablespoons honey
¾ cup (180ml) skim milk
1 medium pear (230g), peeled, grated
1 large peach (220g), cut into wedges
¼ cup (20g) toasted shredded coconut

method

1 Combine muesli, juice, yogurt, dried peach, honey and milk in large bowl. Cover; refrigerate overnight.
2 Stir pear into muesli mixture; serve topped with peach wedges and sprinkled with coconut.

preparation time 25 minutes (plus refrigeration time) serves 4 nutritional count per serving 8.1g total fat (4.1g saturated fat); 2036kJ (487 cal); 82.5g carbohydrate; 13.6g protein; 6.2g fibre

✳ Peach bircher muesli

✳ Oaty apple pikelets

ingredients

2 cups (500ml) skim milk
1 cup (120g) oat bran
½ cup (75g) plain flour
2 tablespoons brown sugar
½ teaspoon mixed spice
2 eggs
1 large apple (200g), peeled, cored, chopped finely
1 tablespoon lemon juice
½ cup (180g) honey
½ cup (120g) low-fat ricotta

method

1 Blend or process milk, bran, flour, sugar, spice and
eggs until smooth; pour into large jug. Stir in apple
and juice, cover; refrigerate 30 minutes (mixture will
separate during refrigeration).
2 Heat large lightly greased frying pan. Stir mixture to
combine; using ¼-cup batter for each pikelet (mixture
will be runny), cook two pikelets at a time, uncovered,
until bubbles appear on the surface. Turn; cook until
browned lightly. Remove pikelets from pan; cover to
keep warm. Repeat with remaining batter to make
12 pikelets.
3 Divide pikelets among plates; top with honey
and ricotta.

preparation time 10 minutes (plus refrigeration time)
cooking time 15 minutes serves 4
nutritional count per serving 7.7g total fat
(3g saturated fat); 2077kJ (497 cal);
84g carbohydrate; 18.6g protein; 6.2g fibre

Breakfast with the lot

preparation time *10 minutes*
cooking time *25 minutes* serves *4*
nutritional count per serving
6.7g total fat (1.9g saturated fat);
702kJ (168 cal); 13g carbohydrate;
12.8g protein; 2.2g fibre

ingredients

2 large egg tomatoes (180g), quartered
4 eggs
4 slices (180g) multigrain bread
60g light ham
50g baby spinach leaves

method

1 Preheat oven to 220°C/200°C fan-forced. Line oven tray with baking paper.
2 Place tomato, cut-side up, on tray; roast, uncovered, about 25 minutes or until softened and browned lightly.
3 Meanwhile place enough water in large shallow frying pan to come halfway up the side; bring to the boil.
4 Break one egg into small bowl, slide into pan; repeat with remaining eggs. When all eggs are in pan, allow water to return to the boil. Cover pan, turn off heat; stand about 4 minutes or until a light film of egg white has set over yolks.
5 Using an egg slide, remove eggs, one at a time, from pan; place egg, still on slide, on absorbent paper-lined saucer to blot up any poaching liquid.
6 Meanwhile, toast bread slices until browned lightly both sides. Serve toast topped with ham, spinach, egg then tomato.

51

✳ Porridge with poached pears and blueberries

ingredients

¾ cup (180ml) hot water
⅓ cup (30g) rolled oats
1 small pear (180g), cored, chopped coarsely
½ cup (125ml) cold water
2 tablespoons blueberries

method

1 Combine the hot water and oats in small saucepan over medium heat; cook, stirring, about 5 minutes or until porridge is thick and creamy.
2 Place pear and the cold water in small saucepan; bring to the boil. Reduce heat, simmer, uncovered, about 5 minutes or until pear softens.
3 Serve porridge topped with pears and 1 tablespoon of the poaching liquid; sprinkle with berries.

preparation time *5 minutes* cooking time *15 minutes* serves *1* nutritional count per serving *2.7g total fat (0.5g saturated fat); 882kJ (211 cal); 43.4g carbohydrate; 3.9g protein; 6.6g fibre*

ingredients

⅓ cup (25g) bran flakes breakfast cereal
⅓ cup (20g) Special K breakfast cereal
⅓ cup (5g) puffed wheat
250g strawberries, hulled
1 cup (280g) low-fat vanilla yogurt
⅓ cup (80ml) passionfruit pulp

method

1 Combine cereals in small bowl.
2 Cut six strawberries in half; reserve. Slice remaining strawberries thinly.
3 Divide half of the cereal mixture among four 1-cup (250ml) serving bowls; divide half of the yogurt, all the strawberry slices and half of the passionfruit pulp among bowls. Continue layering with remaining cereal and yogurt; top with reserved strawberry halves and remaining passionfruit pulp.

preparation time *20 minutes* serves *4*
nutritional count per serving *0.7g total fat (0.1g saturated fat); 543kJ (130 cal); 19g carbohydrate; 8.3g protein; 7.2g fibre*

* Morning trifles

You will need five passionfruit for this recipe.

ingredients

2 cups (180g) rolled oats
1 cup (110g) rolled rice
¼ cup (15g) unprocessed
    wheat bran
¼ cup (50g) pepitas
1 teaspoon ground cinnamon
⅓ cup (120g) honey
1 tablespoon vegetable oil
¾ cup (35g) flaked coconut
⅓ cup (50g) coarsely chopped
    dried apricots
⅓ cup (20g) coarsely chopped
    dried apples
⅓ cup (55g) sultanas
¼ cup (35g) dried cranberries,
    chopped coarsely

method

1 Preheat oven to 180°C/160°C fan-forced.
2 Combine oats and rice in large bowl, then spread evenly onto two oven trays. Roast, uncovered, 5 minutes.
3 Stir bran, pepitas and cinnamon into oat mixture on trays, then drizzle evenly with combined honey and oil; stir to combine. Roast, uncovered, 5 minutes. Add coconut; stir to combine. Roast, uncovered, 5 minutes.
4 Return muesli mixture to large bowl; stir in remaining ingredients. Serve with milk or yogurt.
preparation time *15 minutes* cooking time *15 minutes* serves *6* nutritional count per serving *14.2g total fat (4.2g saturated fat); 1496kJ (358 cal); 46.2g carbohydrate; 6.4g protein; 9.7g fibre*

cook's info

You can double or triple these ingredients and store the muesli in an airtight container in the refrigerator for up to 3 months.

✳ Roasted muesli with dried fruit and honey

*Mini muffin dampers

ingredients

3 cups (450g) self-raising flour
40g butter, chopped coarsely
1¾ cups (430ml) buttermilk
2 tablespoons basil pesto
¾ cup (90g) coarsely grated cheddar cheese
¼ teaspoon sweet paprika
1 tablespoon plain flour

method

1 Preheat oven to 200°C/180°C fan-forced. Grease 12-hole ⅓-cup (80ml) muffin pan.
2 Place self-raising flour in large bowl; rub in butter with fingertips. Using fork, stir in buttermilk to form a soft, sticky dough. Swirl pesto and cheese through; do not overmix.
3 Divide mixture among pan holes; sprinkle with combined paprika and plain flour. Bake 25 minutes.
4 Stand dampers in pan 5 minutes before turning onto a wire rack to cool.

preparation time 10 minutes cooking time 25 minutes makes 12 nutritional count per serving 7.8g total fat (4.3g saturated fat); 924kJ (221 cal); 29.2g carbohydrate; 7.6g protein; 1.5g fibre

cook's info

Sun-dried tomato pesto can also be used.

ingredients

½ cup (25g) flaked coconut
¼ cup (90g) honey
1⅓ cups (330ml) low-fat milk
1 cup (250ml) water
1 cup (90g) rolled oats
¼ cup (40g) finely chopped dried pears
2 tablespoons finely chopped sultanas
2 tablespoons finely chopped dried apricots

method

1 Preheat oven to 180°C/160°C fan-forced. Line shallow medium baking dish with baking paper.
2 Sprinkle coconut into dish; drizzle with 1 tablespoon of the honey. Cook, uncovered, about 5 minutes or until browned lightly. Cool in dish.
3 Meanwhile, stir milk, the water and oats in medium saucepan over medium heat about 10 minutes or until porridge is thick and creamy. Stir in remaining honey and half the dried fruit.
4 Sprinkle porridge with remaining fruit and coconut; serve with warmed milk, if you like.
preparation time *10 minutes* cooking time *15 minutes* serves *4* nutritional count per serving *6.2g total fat (4g saturated fat); 1233kJ (295 cal); 47.7g carbohydrate; 7.3g protein; 4.1g fibre*

Porridge has a low GI rating, meaning it will keep young tummies full for hours.

*Porridge with honeyed coconut and dried fruit

✳ Day-before muffins

ingredients

⅔ cup (100g) coarsely chopped dried apricots
½ cup (95g) coarsely chopped dried figs
1⅓ cups (95g) bran flakes breakfast cereal
1½ cups (375ml) skim milk
1¼ cups (275g) firmly packed brown sugar
1½ tablespoons golden syrup
1¼ cups (185g) self-raising flour
½ cup (60g) pecans, chopped coarsely

method

1 Combine apricot, fig, cereal, milk, sugar and syrup in large bowl; cover, refrigerate overnight.
2 Preheat oven to 200°C/180°C fan-forced. Lightly grease four holes of a six-hole (¾-cup/180ml) texas muffin pan.
3 Stir flour and nuts into apricot mixture. Spoon mixture into pan holes; bake about 30 minutes. Serve muffins hot or cold.

preparation time *15 minutes (plus refrigeration time)*
cooking time *30 minutes* serves *4*
nutritional count per serving *12.9g total fat (1.1g saturated fat); 3214kJ (769 cal); 139.1g carbohydrate; 14.6g protein; 16g fibre*

cook's info

Muffins can be frozen for up to two months.

Serve the muffins dusted with sifted icing sugar and topped with dried apricots, if you like.

These muffins are great when you have overnight guests or friends coming for breakfast as the batter is partially made the day before and refrigerated overnight, needing only a few more minutes of preparation before baking and serving.

2.

The lunchbox

Pizza scrolls

ingredients

2 cups (300g) self-raising flour
1 tablespoon caster sugar
30g cold butter, chopped coarsely
¾ cup (180ml) low-fat milk
¼ cup (70g) tomato paste
2 teaspoons Italian herb blend
100g sliced mild salami, cut into
    thin strips
1 medium green capsicum (200g),
    cut into thin strips
2 cups (200g) coarsely grated
    low-fat cheddar cheese

method

1 Preheat oven to 180°C/160°C fan-forced. Grease 19cm x 29cm slice pan.
2 Place flour and sugar in medium bowl; use fingers to rub butter into flour mixture until it resembles coarse breadcrumbs. Stir in milk; mix to a soft, sticky dough. Knead dough lightly on floured surface. Using rolling pin, roll dough to form 30cm x 40cm rectangle.
3 Using back of large spoon, spread tomato paste all over dough, then sprinkle evenly with herb blend; top with salami, capsicum then cheese.
4 Starting from one of the long sides, roll dough tightly; trim edges. Using serrated knife, cut roll carefully into 12 even slices; place slices, cut-side up, in single layer, in pan. Bake scroll slices, uncovered, about 30 minutes or until browned lightly.

preparation time *20 minutes*
cooking time *30 minutes*
makes *12*
nutritional count per scroll
9.8g total fat
(5.1g saturated fat);
895kJ (214 cal);
20.9g carbohydrate;
10g protein; 1.3g fibre

1. ✳ Tuna and sweet corn sandwich

Combine half a 185g can drained, flaked tuna in springwater, 2 tablespoons rinsed, drained canned sweet corn kernels and 1 tablespoon mayonnaise in a small container. Spread tuna mixture over one slice of bread. Top with ¼ thinly sliced lebanese cucumber and another slice of bread.

preparation time *5 minutes* serves *1*
nutritional count per serving *9.7g total fat (1.7g saturated fat); 1379kJ (330 cal); 34.4g carbohydrate; 24.4g protein; 3g fibre*

2. ✳ Cheese and salad sandwich

Combine 200g low-fat cottage cheese, ⅓ cup coarsely grated reduced-fat cheddar cheese, 1 cup shredded baby spinach leaves, 1 thinly sliced green onion, 1 finely grated small carrot, 1 tablespoon roasted sesame seeds and 2 teaspoons lemon juice in medium bowl. Sandwich 30g mesclun and cheese mixture between 8 slices of wholemeal bread.

preparation time *5 minutes* serves *4*
nutritional count per sandwich *6g total fat (2.3g saturated fat); 911kJ (218 cal); 20.9g carbohydrate; 17.5g protein; 4.5g fibre*

3. ✳ Egg salad sandwich

Combine 6 finely chopped hard-boiled eggs, 1 finely chopped celery stalk, 1 finely sliced green onion, 2 tablespoons finely grated parmesan cheese and ¼ cup low-fat mayonnaise in medium bowl. Sandwich egg mixture, 1 cup shredded iceberg lettuce and 2 sliced egg tomatoes between 8 slices of white bread.

preparation time *10 minutes* serves *4*
nutritional count per sandwich *13.6g total fat (4g saturated fat); 1622kJ (388 cal); 44.8g carbohydrate; 19.5g protein; 3.7g fibre*

Filling can be stored, in an airtight container, in the refrigerator for up to two days.

4. ✳ Hummus and cucumber sandwich

Spread one slice of bread with 1 tablespoon hummus; top with ¼ thinly sliced lebanese cucumber and another slice of bread.

preparation time *5 minutes* serves *1*
nutritional count per serving *5g total fat (0.9g saturated fat); 769kJ (184 cal); 27.6g carbohydrate; 6.8g protein; 3.8g fibre*

1

2

3

4

65

1

3

2

4

1. ✳ Lavash wrap

Spread one piece wholemeal lavash with
¼ small avocado and 1 teaspoon tahini. Place
½ cup coarsely grated uncooked beetroot,
⅓ cup coarsely grated uncooked pumpkin,
¼ thinly sliced small red capsicum, 40g thinly
sliced button mushrooms and ¼ small thinly
sliced red onion on long side of bread; roll
to enclose filling, cut in half.

preparation time *15 minutes* serves *2*
nutritional count per serving *6.7g total fat*
(1.3g saturated fat); 769kJ (184 cal);
22.3g carbohydrate; 6.1g protein; 5.g fibre

2. Mediterranean tuna baguette

Cook 1 diced medium potato until tender; drain.
Shake 2 tablespoons olive oil, 1 tablespoon red
wine vinegar and 1 teaspoon dijon mustard
together in screw-top jar. Combine potato and
dressing with 1 tablespoon finely chopped
black olives, 1 finely chopped seeded medium
tomato and a drained 185g can tuna in
springwater in medium bowl. Halve 2 small
french sticks crossways then split in half.
Sandwich 30g mesclun, 2 sliced hard-boiled
eggs and tuna mixture between bread pieces.

preparation time *5 minutes*
cooking time *10 minutes* serves *4*
nutritional count per serving *15.7g total fat*
(2.9g saturated fat); 1781kJ (426 cal);
47.9g carbohydrate; 20.9g protein; 4.2g fibre

Filling can be stored, in an airtight container,
in the refrigerator for up to two days.

3. ✳ Chicken burritos

Combine 1¼ cups coarsely chopped cooked
chicken, ¼ cup mayonnaise and ¼ cup sour
cream in medium bowl. Divide chicken mixture,
1 cup finely shredded lettuce, 2 small finely
chopped tomatoes and ½ cup coarsely grated
cheddar cheese among 3 x 20cm flour tortillas;
roll securely to enclose filling. Cut tortillas
in half.

preparation time *10 minutes* serves *6*
nutritional count per serving *15g total fat*
(6g saturated fat); 1007kJ (241 cal);
15.6g carbohydrate; 11.2g protein; 1.5g fibre

Filling can be stored, in an airtight container,
in the refrigerator for up to two days.

4. Niçoise salad

Cook 100g quartered baby new potatoes and
50g halved green beans, separately, until
tender. Rinse under cold water; drain. Combine
potato and beans with a 95g can drained and
flaked tuna in springwater, 1 quartered hard-
boiled egg, 1 tablespoon each seeded black
olives and coarsely chopped fresh flat-leaf
parsley in medium bowl. Pack salad with half
a lemon.

preparation time *5 minutes*
cooking time *5 minutes* serves *1*
nutritional count per serving *7.8g total fat*
(2.4g saturated fat); 1179kJ (282 cal);
20.3g carbohydrate; 29.7g protein; 4.9g fibre

Top Tip

Keep their lunch cool at school in an insulated lunch bag. You can also freeze drinks and use them as ice packs to keep contents cool; as they melt they will provide an icy drink for later.

1. Chicken salad sandwiches

Combine 1½ cups finely chopped cooked chicken, 2 tablespoons finely chopped pecans, 4 thinly sliced green onions, ¼ cup low-fat mayonnaise and ½ finely chopped trimmed celery stalk in medium bowl. Spread 3 slices of wholemeal bread with the chicken mixture; divide 60g rocket evenly over slices then top each with another slice of wholemeal bread.
preparation time *10 minutes* serves *3*
nutritional count per serving *19.2g total fat (3.2g saturated fat); 1689kJ (409 cal); 30.9g carbohydrate; 25.4g protein; 2.9g fibre*

Filling can be stored, in an airtight container, in the refrigerator for up to two days. Wholemeal and multigrain breads contain more fibre than white-flour breads, and also have more flavour.

2. Beef, cheese and carrot sandwich

Combine ½ small coarsely grated carrot, 2 tablespoons spreadable cream cheese and 2 tablespoons finely shredded iceberg lettuce in a small bowl. Spread half the carrot mixture on one slice of white bread; top with ¼ cup finely chopped roast beef, remaining carrot mixture and another slice of bread.
preparation time *10 minutes* serves *1*
nutritional count per serving *15.7g total fat (9.1g saturated fat); 1296kJ (310 cal); 25.1g carbohydrate; 15.7g protein; 2.9g fibre*

3. *Turkey and cream cheese roll-ups

Spread one piece of lavash bread with 1 tablespoon spreadable cream cheese. Place 3 slices smoked turkey, 3 cheese slices, 3 iceberg lettuce leaves and 1 thinly sliced small egg tomato on bread; roll tightly then cut in half.
preparation time *5 minutes* serves *2*
nutritional count per serving *13.9g total fat (8g saturated fat); 1187kJ (284 cal); 19g carbohydrate; 20g protein; 1.9g fibre*

4. Pea, ricotta, mint and spinach sandwich

Boil, steam or microwave ¾ cup frozen peas until tender; drain. Cool, then lightly crush with a fork. Combine pea mash with ¾ cup ricotta cheese, ¼ cup lemon juice and ¼ cup finely chopped fresh mint. Spread pea mixture evenly over three slices of soy and linseed bread; divide 60g baby spinach leaves evenly over slices then top each with another slice of bread.
preparation time *5 minutes*
cooking time *5 minutes* serves *3*
nutritional count per serving *9.7g total fat (4.6g saturated fat); 1417kJ (339 cal); 42.2g carbohydrate; 17g protein; 6.9g fibre*

Filling can be stored, in an airtight container, in the refrigerator for up to three days.

1

3

2

4

ingredients

½ cup (85g) polenta
½ cup (125ml) low-fat milk
2 rindless bacon rashers (195g), chopped finely
4 green onions, chopped finely
1½ cups (225g) self-raising flour
1 tablespoon caster sugar
310g can corn kernels, drained
125g can creamed corn
100g butter, melted
2 eggs, beaten lightly
50g piece low-fat cheddar cheese
¼ cup (30g) coarsely grated low-fat cheddar cheese

method

1 Preheat oven to 200°C/180°C fan-forced. Oil 12-hole (⅓-cup/80ml) muffin pan.
2 Mix polenta and milk in small bowl; cover, stand 20 minutes.
3 Meanwhile, cook bacon in heated small frying pan, stirring, about 2 minutes. Add onion; cook, stirring, 2 minutes. Remove pan from heat; cool bacon mixture about 5 minutes.
4 Sift flour and sugar into large bowl; stir in corn kernels, creamed corn and bacon mixture. Add melted butter, egg and polenta mixture; mix muffin batter only until just combined.
5 Spoon 1 tablespoon of the batter into each pan hole. Cut the piece of cheese into 12 equal-sized pieces (about a 3cm cube); place one piece in the middle of the batter. Divide remaining batter among pan holes; sprinkle with grated cheese.
6 Bake, uncovered, about 20 minutes or until muffins are well-risen. Turn muffins onto wire rack.
preparation time *20 minutes (plus standing time)*
cooking time *25 minutes* makes *12*
nutritional count per muffin *13.3g total fat*
(7.4g saturated fat); 1112kJ (266 cal);
25.7g carbohydrate; 9.8g protein; 1.9g fibre

Mix batter just enough to combine the ingredients, as overmixing produces tough, heavy muffins. Corn is very nutritious, and is especially high in iron, necessary for healthy red blood cells.

Cheese, corn and bacon muffins

3.

After-school snacks

* Noodle and vegetable rolls

ingredients

60g rice vermicelli noodles
½ medium carrot (60g), grated coarsely
½ small wombok (350g), shredded finely
1 tablespoon fish sauce
1 tablespoon brown sugar
¼ cup (60ml) lemon juice
12 x 17cm-square rice paper sheets
12 large fresh mint leaves
sweet chilli dipping sauce
¼ cup (60ml) sweet chilli sauce
1 tablespoon fish sauce
1 tablespoon lime juice

preparation time *20 minutes*
cooking time *5 minutes*
makes *12 rolls*
nutritional count per roll
0.2g total fat (0g saturated fat);
188kJ (45 cal); 9g carbohydrate;
1.4g protein; 0.8g fibre
nutritional count per tablespoon
dipping sauce *0.4g total fat*
(0.1g saturated fat); 71kJ
(17 cal); 2.7g carbohydrate;
0.4g protein; 0.6g fibre

method

1 Place noodles in medium heatproof bowl, cover with boiling water; stand until just tender, drain. Using kitchen scissors, cut noodles into random lengths.
2 Place noodles in medium bowl with carrot, wombok, sauce, sugar and juice; toss gently to combine.
3 To assemble rolls, place one sheet of rice paper in medium bowl of warm water until just softened; lift sheet carefully from water, placing it on a tea-towel-covered board with a corner point facing towards you. Place a little of the vegetable filling and one mint leaf vertically along centre of sheet; fold top and bottom corners over filling then roll sheet from side to side to enclose filling. Repeat with remaining rice paper sheets, vegetable filling and mint leaves.
4 Combine ingredients for sweet chilli dipping sauce in small bowl. Serve rolls with sweet chilli dipping sauce.

ingredients

¼ cup (60ml) olive oil
2 cloves garlic, crushed
4 slices (180g) wholegrain bread
1 medium avocado (250g), chopped coarsely
100g bocconcini cheese, chopped coarsely
¼ cup (40g) seeded black olives, chopped coarsely
1 tablespoon lemon juice
2 medium tomatoes (300g), chopped coarsely

method

1 Preheat grill.
2 Combine half the oil and half the garlic in small bowl. Brush both sides of bread with garlic oil; toast under grill until browned lightly both sides.
3 Combine avocado, cheese, olives, juice, tomato and remaining oil and garlic in medium bowl.
4 Cut toasts in half; top with avocado mixture.

preparation time *15 minutes* cooking time *5 minutes* serves *4* nutritional count per serving *1693kJ (405 cal); 28.8g total fat (6.8g saturated fat); 24.4g carbohydrate; 10.1g protein; 4.5g fibre*

Avocado, olive and bocconcini bruschetta

✳ Hoisin and barbecued chicken rolls

ingredients
½ lebanese cucumber (65g)
½ medium carrot (60g)
12 x 17cm square rice paper sheets
2 tablespoons hoisin sauce
1¼ cups (200g) finely shredded
    barbecued chicken meat
50g snow peas, trimmed, sliced thinly

method
1 Using vegetable peeler, slice cucumber and carrot into ribbons.
2 To assemble rolls, place one sheet of rice paper in medium bowl of warm water until just softened; lift sheet carefully from water, placing it on a tea-towel-covered board with a corner point facing towards you. Place a little of the sauce and chicken vertically along centre of sheet; top with a little of the cucumber, carrot and snow peas. Fold corner point facing you up over filling; roll rice paper sheet side to side to enclose filling. Repeat with remaining rice paper sheets and filling ingredients.
preparation time *20 minutes* makes *12*
nutritional count per serving *1.1g total fat
(0.3g saturated fat); 184kJ (44 cal);
5g carbohydrate; 3.1g protein; 0.8g fibre*

1. ✳ Ham, cheese and tomato melts

Preheat grill. Spread 2 teaspoons tomato chutney over two slices of white bread; top each slice with half a slice of ham, a quarter of a thinly sliced tomato, and one slice of swiss cheese. Place under grill about 5 minutes or until cheese melts.

preparation time *5 minutes* makes *2*
nutritional count per serving *7.1g total fat (4g saturated fat); 690kJ (165 cal); 14.4g carbohydrate; 10.1g protein; 1.3g fibre*

2. ✳ Cheese, tomato and bacon open sandwich

Cook one trimmed bacon rasher in a small frying pan until browned; chop coarsely. Layer one slice of fat-reduced cheddar cheese, half a thinly sliced medium egg tomato and the bacon pieces on one slice of white bread.

preparation time *5 minutes*
cooking time *5 minutes* makes *1*
nutritional count per serving *10.9g total fat (5.2g saturated fat); 878kJ (210 cal); 11.8g carbohydrate; 15.9g protein; 1.1g fibre*

3. ✳ Salami, tomato and olive open sandwich

Spread half a white bread roll with 1 teaspoon butter; layer with two slices of danish salami, half a thinly sliced medium egg tomato, 1 tablespoon sliced seeded black olives and 1 tablespoon coarsely grated pizza cheese.

preparation time *5 minutes* makes *1*
nutritional count per serving *12.2g total fat (5.6g saturated fat); 1137kJ (272 cal); 29.6g carbohydrate; 9.7g protein; 2.4g fibre*

4. ✳ Tomato, spinach and cheese melts

Preheat grill. Layer 60g baby spinach leaves, two thinly sliced medium tomatoes and ⅔ cup grated cheddar cheese between four english muffins or crumpets. Place under grill about 5 minutes or until cheese melts.

preparation time *10 minutes*
cooking time *5 minutes* makes *4*
nutritional count per serving *7.8g total fat (4.5g saturated fat); 949kJ (227 cal); 24.9g carbohydrate; 12.5g protein; 3.2g fibre*

1 3
2 4

✳ Pumpkin and fetta pizza

ingredients

50g piece pumpkin
1 teaspoon olive oil
1 pocket pitta bread (85g)
2 tablespoons bottled tomato pasta sauce
25g reduced-fat fetta cheese, crumbled
2 teaspoons finely chopped fresh mint

method

1 Preheat oven to 180°C/160°C fan-forced.
2 Using vegetable peeler, slice pumpkin into thin strips. Combine pumpkin and oil in small bowl.
3 Spread pitta with sauce; top with pumpkin and cheese. Cook about 15 minutes or until pumpkin is tender. Serve sprinkled with mint.

preparation time *10 minutes* cooking time *15 minutes* serves *1* nutritional count per serving *10.7g total fat (3.4g saturated fat); 1576kJ (377 cal); 51.6g carbohydrate; 16.1g protein; 3.9g fibre*

ingredients

3 large button mushrooms, chopped finely
1 tablespoon basil pesto
1 pocket pitta bread (85g)
25g ham, chopped finely
1 tablespoon pizza cheese
2 tablespoons low-fat cottage cheese
1 tablespoon finely chopped fresh flat-leaf parsley

method

1 Preheat oven to 180°C/160°C fan-forced.
2 Combine mushrooms and pesto in small bowl. Spread pitta with mushroom mixture; top with ham and cheeses. Cook about 15 minutes or until cheese melts. Sprinkle parsley over pizza just before serving.

preparation time *5 minutes* cooking time *15 minutes* serves *1* nutritional count per serving *15.6g total fat (5.4g saturated fat); 1848kJ (442 cal); 45.4g carbohydrate; 27.9g protein; 3.8g fibre*

*Pesto, ham and mushroom pizza

Top Tip

Have healthy after-school snacks already prepared for when kids get home; this will stop them filling up on highly processed foods.

ingredients

1 pocket pitta bread (85g)
¼ cup (60g) canned refried beans
¼ small red capsicum (35g), chopped finely
2 teaspoons sweet chilli sauce
2 tablespoons pizza cheese
1 green onion, sliced thinly

method

1 Preheat oven to 180°C/160°C fan-forced.
2 Spread pitta with beans; top with capsicum, sauce and cheese. Cook about 15 minutes or until cheese melts. Sprinkle onion over pizza just before serving.
preparation time 5 minutes cooking time 15 minutes serves 1 nutritional count per serving 9.5g total fat (4.7g saturated fat); 1689kJ (404 cal); 54.7g carbohydrate; 21g protein; 6.6g fibre

✳Mexican pizza

*Ham, egg and cheese toastie

ingredients

2 slices wholemeal bread (90g)
1 tablespoon barbecue sauce
30g shaved ham
1 hard-boiled egg, sliced thinly
¼ cup (30g) coarsely grated reduced-fat
    cheddar cheese

method

1 Spread bread with sauce; sandwich ham, egg and
cheese between bread slices.

2 Toast in sandwich press until golden brown.
preparation time *5 minutes* cooking time *5 minutes*
makes *1* nutritional count per serving *16.1g total fat
(6.9g saturated fat); 1898kJ (454 cal); 44.3g carbohydrate;
29.7g protein; 5.9g fibre*

✳ Bruschetta fingers

ingredients

1 small turkish bread roll (160g)
2 teaspoons sun-dried tomato pesto
6 cherry tomatoes, quartered
30g cherry bocconcini cheese, sliced thinly
1 tablespoon finely chopped fresh flat-leaf parsley

method

1 Split bread in half; toast, cut-side up, then cut into fingers.
2 Spread toasted sides with pesto; top with tomato and
cheese then sprinkle with parsley.
preparation time *5 minutes* cooking time *5 minutes*
serves *1* nutritional count per serving 14.5*g total fat
(4.7g saturated fat); 2358kJ (569 cal); 81.9g carbohydrate;
22.5g protein; 6.1g fibre*

ingredients

1 small turkish bread roll (160g)
1 tablespoon cranberry sauce
30g shaved turkey
10g shaved reduced-fat jarlsberg cheese
10g baby spinach leaves

method

1 Split bread in half. Spread sauce onto cut sides then sandwich turkey, cheese and spinach between pieces.
2 Toast in sandwich press until golden brown.
preparation time *5 minutes* cooking time *5 minutes* makes *1* nutritional count per serving *9.5g total fat (2.8g saturated fat); 2207kJ (528 cal); 80.9g carbohydrate; 26.2g protein; 4.4g fibre*

*Turkey on toasted turkish

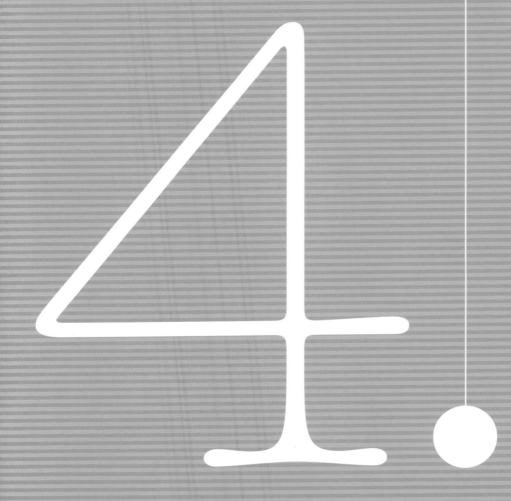

4.
Family dinners

Cheesy-vegie pasta bake

ingredients

375g penne
300g broccoli, cut into florets
500g cauliflower, cut into florets
2 teaspoons vegetable oil
1 large brown onion (200g), chopped finely
1 teaspoon mustard powder
1 teaspoon sweet paprika
¼ cup (35g) plain flour
1½ cups (375ml) low-fat milk
420g can tomato soup
400g can diced tomatoes
1½ cups (180g) coarsely grated reduced-fat
    cheddar cheese
2 tablespoons finely chopped fresh flat-leaf parsley

preparation time *15 minutes*
cooking time *20 minutes* serves *6*
nutritional count per serving
10.9g total fat (5.4g saturated fat);
1952kJ (467 cal); 62.3g carbohydrate;
25.5g protein; 7.4g fibre

method

1 Cook pasta in large saucepan of boiling water, uncovered, until just tender; drain. Cover to keep warm.
2 Meanwhile, boil, steam or microwave broccoli and cauliflower until tender; drain. Cover to keep warm.
3 Heat oil in same large saucepan; cook onion, stirring, until softened. Add mustard, paprika and flour; cook, stirring, over low heat, 2 minutes. Gradually stir in milk and soup; stir over heat until mixture boils and thickens. Add undrained tomatoes; cook, stirring, until mixture is hot.
4 Preheat grill.
5 Stir pasta, broccoli, cauliflower and 1 cup of the cheese into tomato mixture. Divide pasta mixture among six 1-cup (250ml) flameproof dishes, sprinkle with remaining cheese; grill until cheese melts and is browned lightly. Sprinkle pasta bake with parsley just before serving.

Veal with potato pea mash

Veal can be crumbed several hours ahead; store, covered, in the refrigerator.

serving suggestion

Serve veal with a contrasting coloured vegetable such as boiled or steamed carrots, corn on the cob, or oven-roasted tomatoes.

preparation time *10 minutes*
cooking time *20 minutes* serves *4*
nutritional count per serving
4g total fat (0.9g saturated fat);
2174kJ (520 cal); 74.5g carbohydrate;
40.2g protein; 9.9g fibre

ingredients

450g veal steaks
⅓ cup (50g) plain flour
1 egg white, beaten lightly
2 tablespoons skim milk
1 cup (160g) corn flake crumbs
1 teaspoon finely grated lemon rind
2 tablespoons finely chopped fresh flat-leaf parsley
cooking-oil spray
4 medium potatoes (800g)
¼ cup (60ml) buttermilk
¾ cup (180ml) chicken stock
2 cups (250g) frozen peas
1 lemon, cut into 8 wedges

method

1 Preheat oven to 240°C/220°C fan-forced.
2 Cut each steak in half. Toss veal in flour; shake away excess flour. Coat veal in combined egg white and milk, then in combined crumbs, rind and parsley.
3 Place veal, in single layer, on oiled oven tray; spray lightly with cooking-oil spray. Bake veal, uncovered, about 5 minutes or until cooked through. Stand veal 5 minutes then slice thickly.
4 Meanwhile, boil, steam or microwave potatoes until soft; drain. Mash potatoes with buttermilk in medium bowl; cover to keep warm.
5 Place stock in medium saucepan; bring to the boil. Add peas; cook, uncovered, until stock reduces by half. Blend or process until pea mixture is almost pureed.
6 Gently swirl pea mixture into potato mash to give marbled effect. Divide potato and pea mash among plates; top with veal. Serve with lemon.

95

✳ Light & spicy crumbed chicken

ingredients

12 chicken tenderloins (900g)
⅓ cup (50g) plain flour
2 egg whites, beaten lightly
⅓ cup (35g) packaged breadcrumbs
⅓ cup (55g) corn flake crumbs
2 teaspoons garlic salt
1 teaspoon lemon pepper

method

1 Toss chicken in flour; shake away excess flour. Coat chicken in egg, then in combined remaining ingredients. Cover, refrigerate 15 minutes.
2 Preheat oven to 220°C/200°C fan-forced.
3 Place chicken, in single layer, on oven tray; bake, uncovered, about 15 minutes or until cooked through.

preparation time *15 minutes (plus refrigeration time)*
cooking time *15 minutes* serves *4*
nutritional count per serving *5.7g total fat
(1.4g saturated fat); 1538kJ (368 cal);
22.2g carbohydrate; 55.8g protein; 1.1g fibre*

ingredients

500g fresh wide rice noodles
1 tablespoon sesame oil
500g chicken breast fillets, sliced thinly
250g oyster mushrooms, sliced thinly
¼ cup (60ml) oyster sauce
1 tablespoon fish sauce
1 tablespoon white sugar
2 teaspoons sambal oelek
250g baby spinach leaves
¼ cup coarsely chopped fresh coriander

method

1 Rinse noodles in strainer under hot water. Separate noodles with fork; drain.
2 Heat oil in wok; stir-fry chicken, in batches, until browned all over and cooked through.
3 Add mushrooms to wok; stir-fry until just tender. Return chicken to wok with noodles, sauces, sugar and sambal; stir-fry until heated through.
4 Remove wok from heat. Add spinach and coriander; toss to combine.
   preparation time *10 minutes* cooking time *15 minutes* serves *4* nutritional count per serving *8.6g total fat (1.4g saturated fat); 1572kJ (376 cal); 36.4g carbohydrate; 35.2g protein; 5.3g fibre*

Chicken, vegetable and rice noodle stir-fry

Crumbed fish with warm tomato salad

ingredients

cooking-oil spray
1 medium red onion (170g)
250g cherry tomatoes
¼ cup (60ml) white wine vinegar
2 cloves garlic, crushed
⅓ cup (55g) corn flake crumbs
1 teaspoon ground cumin
1 teaspoon sweet paprika
1 teaspoon ground turmeric
4 firm white fish fillets (800g)
¼ cup (35g) plain flour
2 egg whites, beaten lightly
150g baby spinach leaves
¼ cup (50g) drained capers

method

1 Preheat oven to 220°C/200°C fan-forced.
2 Spray oven tray lightly with cooking-oil spray. Cut onion into thin wedges. Place onion and tomatoes on tray; drizzle with combined vinegar and garlic. Roast, uncovered, about 20 minutes or until tomatoes are softened.
3 Combine crumbs and spices in small bowl.
4 Meanwhile, coat fish in flour; shake away excess flour. Dip fish in egg white, coat in crumb mixture. Spray fish both sides with cooking-oil spray; cook, uncovered, in heated large frying pan until browned both sides and cooked through.
5 Combine spinach and capers in large bowl with tomato and onion mixture; serve with fish.

You can use flathead, ling, snapper, bream or any other firm white fish in this recipe.

preparation time *15 minutes*
cooking time *25 minutes* serves *4*
nutritional count per serving
4.9g total fat (1.3g saturated fat);
1321kJ (316 cal); 23g carbohydrate;
42.4g protein; 3.7g fibre

ingredients

2 teaspoons peanut oil
1 medium brown onion (150g), chopped coarsely
2 cloves garlic, crushed
2cm piece fresh ginger (10g), grated
300g lean pork mince
1 trimmed celery stalk (100g), sliced thickly
1 small red capsicum (150g), chopped coarsely
1 large zucchini (150g), chopped coarsely
4 cups (600g) cooked Doongara rice
¾ cup (90g) frozen peas, thawed
¼ cup (60ml) japanese soy sauce
2 green onions, sliced thinly

method

1 Heat oil in wok; stir-fry brown onion, garlic and ginger until onion has just softened. Add pork; stir-fry until brown and cooked through.
2 Add celery, capsicum and zucchini; stir-fry until just tender. Add rice, peas and sauce; stir-fry until hot. Toss green onion through fried rice just before serving.
preparation time *10 minutes* cooking time *10 minutes* serves 4 nutritional count per serving *8.2g total fat (2.4g saturated fat); 1527kJ (365 cal); 19.6g carbohydrate; 28.3g protein; 4.2g fibre*

Also known as "Clever Rice", Doongara rice is a white, long-grain, Australian-grown rice that can be found in supermarkets. You need to cook about 1½ cups of rice for this recipe.

Cold rice, cooked the day before you intend to prepare the recipe, is best for this dish; the individual grains remain separate from one another and won't get mushy when they're reheated in the wok. Spread the cooked rice on a tray and allow to cool before covering and refrigerating overnight.

Fried rice

ingredients

1 small red onion (100g), halved
500g lean beef mince
½ cup (125ml) barbecue sauce
1 tablespoon tomato sauce
4 thin slices fresh pineapple (150g)
4 hamburger buns (360g)
1½ cups finely shredded iceberg lettuce
1 large tomato (220g), sliced thinly
225g can beetroot slices, drained

method

1 Chop half the onion finely; cut remaining half into four slices.
2 Combine mince, 1 tablespoon of the barbecue sauce, tomato sauce and chopped onion in medium bowl. Shape mixture into four patties.
3 Cook pineapple slices and onion slices on heated oiled grill plate until pineapple is browned. Cook patties.
4 Preheat grill. Split buns; toast, cut-sides up, under grill.
5 Spread remaining barbecue sauce on bun bases; layer ingredients between bun halves.

preparation time *15 minutes* cooking time *20 minutes* serves *4* nutritional count per serving *12.3g total fat (4.1g saturated fat); 2337kJ (559 cal); 71.8g carbohydrate; 35.7g protein; 6.9g fibre*

Beef burgers

✳Chinese barbecued wings

ingredients

1kg chicken wings
1 tablespoon peanut oil
1 tablespoon soy sauce
2 tablespoons char sui sauce
1 teaspoon five-spice powder

method

1 Cut wings into three pieces at joints; discard tips. Combine oil, sauces and five-spice powder in large bowl. Add chicken; toss to coat all over in mixture. Cover; refrigerate 3 hours or overnight.
2 Preheat oven to 220°C/200°C fan-forced.
3 Place chicken, in single layer, on oiled wire rack set inside large shallow baking dish; brush remaining marinade over chicken. Roast, uncovered, about 30 minutes or until chicken is well browned and cooked through.
   preparation time *10 minutes (plus refrigeration time)*
   cooking time *30 minutes* serves *4*
   nutritional count per serving *13g total fat
   (3.6g saturated fat); 1150kJ (275 cal);
   2.7g carbohydrate; 36.7g protein; 6g fibre*

*Chicken vegetable soup with croutons

ingredients

1 tablespoon olive oil
1 medium brown onion (150g), chopped finely
1 clove garlic, crushed
2 medium tomatoes (300g), chopped finely
400g chicken breast fillets, sliced thinly
450g piece pumpkin, finely chopped
2 litres (8 cups) chicken stock
2 slices wholemeal bread (90g)
420g can borlotti beans, rinsed, drained
150g broccoli, cut into florets
½ cup (40g) coarsely grated parmesan cheese

method

1 Preheat oven to 180°C/160°C fan-forced.
2 Heat half the oil in large saucepan; cook onion, garlic and tomato, stirring, until onion softens. Add chicken, pumpkin and stock; bring to the boil. Reduce heat; simmer, uncovered, about 10 minutes or until pumpkin is almost tender.
3 Meanwhile, cut bread into shapes with cutter; combine bread and remaining oil in small bowl. Place bread, in single layer, on oven tray; toast, in oven, until croutons are crisp.
4 Add beans and broccoli to soup; cook, uncovered, about 3 minutes or until heated through.
5 Serve soup topped with croutons and sprinkled with cheese.

preparation time *20 minutes*
cooking time *25 minutes* serves *6*
nutritional count per serving
11.4g total fat (4g saturated fat);
1434kJ (343 cal); 27.7g carbohydrate;
29.7g protein; 5.6g fibre

You can use any shaped cutter you like for the croutons, or simply cut the bread into cubes.

Stir-fried pork with buk choy and rice noodles

ingredients

¼ cup (60ml) oyster sauce
2 tablespoons light soy sauce
2 tablespoons sweet sherry
1 tablespoon brown sugar
1 clove garlic, crushed
1 star anise, crushed
pinch five-spice powder
400g fresh rice noodles
2 teaspoons sesame oil
600g pork fillets, sliced thinly
700g baby buk choy, chopped coarsely

method

1 Combine sauces, sherry, sugar, garlic, star anise and five-spice in small jug.
2 Place noodles in large heatproof bowl, cover with boiling water; separate with fork, drain.
3 Heat oil in wok; stir-fry pork, in batches, until cooked through. Return pork to wok with sauce mixture, noodles and buk choy; stir-fry until buk choy is wilted.
preparation time *10 minutes* cooking time *10 minutes* serves *4* nutritional count per serving *6.7g total fat (1.6g saturated fat); 1492kJ (357 cal); 31.6g carbohydrate; 37.9g protein; 2.9g fibre*

ingredients

1 clove garlic, crushed
80g lean beef mince
½ teaspoon chilli powder
¼ teaspoon ground cumin
300g can kidney beans, rinsed, drained
2 tablespoons tomato paste
½ cup (125ml) water
1 medium tomato (150g), chopped coarsely
4 taco shells
¼ small iceberg lettuce, shredded finely
salsa cruda
½ lebanese cucumber (65g), seeded, chopped finely
½ small red onion (40g), chopped finely
1 small tomato (90g), seeded, chopped finely
1 teaspoon sweet chilli sauce

method

1 Preheat oven to 180°C/160°C fan-forced.
2 Heat large oiled frying pan; cook garlic and beef, stirring, until beef is browned all over. Add chilli, cumin, beans, paste, the water and tomato; cook, covered, over low heat about 15 minutes or until mixture thickens slightly.
3 Meanwhile, place taco shells upside-down on oven tray; heat, uncovered, 5 minutes or until warmed through.
4 Make salsa cruda.
5 To serve, fill taco shells with beef mixture, lettuce and salsa cruda.
   salsa cruda Combine ingredients in small bowl.
   preparation time *15 minutes* cooking time *20 minutes*
   serves *4* nutritional count per serving *4.6g total fat*
   (1g saturated fat); 654kJ (156 cal); 18.4g carbohydrate;
   10.1g protein; 6.8g fibre

Beef and bean tacos

Minestrone with meatballs

ingredients

1 tablespoon olive oil
1 large brown onion (200g),
    chopped finely
2 cloves garlic, crushed
1 large carrot (180g), cut into
    1cm pieces
2 trimmed celery stalks (200g),
    cut into 1cm pieces
2 tablespoons tomato paste
2 cups (500ml) chicken stock
400g can crushed tomatoes
1½ cups (375ml) water
425g can white beans, rinsed, drained
½ cup (180g) small pasta shells
2 tablespoons finely chopped
    fresh oregano
meatballs
500g lean beef mince
1 small brown onion (80g),
    chopped finely
2 cloves garlic, crushed
½ cup (35g) stale breadcrumbs
1 egg
1 tablespoon olive oil

method

1 Make meatballs.
2 Heat oil in large saucepan; cook onion and garlic, stirring, until onion softens. Add carrot and celery; cook, stirring, about 5 minutes or until vegetables are tender. Add paste; cook, stirring, 2 minutes.
3 Add stock, undrained tomatoes and the water; bring to the boil. Add meatballs, beans and pasta, reduce heat; simmer, uncovered, about 20 minutes or until meatballs are cooked through. Serve soup sprinkled with oregano.
meatballs Combine mince, onion, garlic, breadcrumbs and egg in medium bowl; roll level tablespoons of mixture into balls. Heat oil in large frying pan; cook meatballs, in batches, until browned.

preparation time *30 minutes*
cooking time *45 minutes* serves *6*
nutritional count per serving *14.6g total fat
(3.9g saturated fat); 1572kJ (376 cal);
33.4g carbohydrate; 26.2g protein; 5.6g fibre*

Everybody loves meatballs so your kids won't complain about having to eat their vegetables when they see these yummy meatballs in their bowls. Many varieties of cooked white beans are available canned, among them cannellini, butter and haricot, any of which is suitable for this recipe.

ingredients

100g rice stick noodles
2 teaspoons vegetable oil
500g lean chicken mince
1 medium red onion (170g), chopped finely
1 tablespoon curry powder
1 large carrot (180g), chopped finely
2 tablespoons oyster sauce
2 tablespoons char siu sauce
½ small wombok (350g), shredded coarsely
100g snow peas, sliced lengthways
8 large wombok leaves

method

1 Place noodles in medium heatproof bowl, cover with boiling water; stand 3 minutes, drain. Cut into random lengths.
2 Heat oil in wok; stir-fry mince and onion until mince changes colour. Add curry powder; stir-fry until fragrant. Add carrot; stir-fry until carrot softens.
3 Add sauces, wombok and peas to wok; stir-fry about 2 minutes or until vegetables soften.
4 Divide wombok leaves among serving bowls. Toss noodles with mince mixture; divide among wombok cups.

preparation time 10 minutes cooking time 10 minutes serves 4 nutritional count per serving 13.7g total fat (3.4g saturated fat); 1572kJ (376 cal); 29.9g carbohydrate; 29.7g protein; 6.3g fibre

Remove eight large outer leaves from trimmed wombok, before shredding.

Chicken sang choy bow

The flavour of the bolognese
will improve if it is made a day
ahead; reheat just before serving.

Fettuccine bolognese

ingredients

1 small brown onion (80g), chopped finely
2 cloves garlic, crushed
1 small carrot (70g), chopped finely
1 trimmed celery stalk (100g), chopped finely
400g lean beef mince
2 cups (500ml) bottled tomato pasta sauce
½ cup (125ml) beef stock
375g fettuccine
2 tablespoons coarsely chopped fresh flat-leaf parsley

method

1 Cook onion and garlic in heated large oiled frying pan, stirring, until onion softens. Add carrot and celery; cook, stirring, until vegetables are just tender.
2 Add beef; cook, stirring, until changed in colour. Add sauce and stock; bring to the boil then simmer, uncovered, about 15 minutes or until mixture thickens slightly.
3 Meanwhile, cook pasta in large saucepan of boiling water, uncovered, until just tender; drain.
4 Serve fettuccine topped with bolognese sauce and sprinkled with parsley.
preparation time *5 minutes* cooking time *25 minutes*
serves *4* nutritional count per serving *9.2g total fat
(3.3g saturated fat); 1522kJ (364 cal); 81.3g carbohydrate;
34g protein; 7.4g fibre*

serving suggestion Serve with a green salad and ciabatta bread.

Top Tip

Present food to children so that it's attractive, fun and interesting. If food is bland, and meal-times boring, kids will be more attracted to the food in TV commercials.

preparation time *30 minutes*
cooking time *20 minutes* serves *8*
nutritional count per serving
12.1g total fat (5.7g saturated fat);
1555kJ (372 cal); 28g carbohydrate;
35.1g protein; 4.3g fibre

Beef fajitas

ingredients

800g trimmed beef rump steak
1 large red capsicum (350g), sliced thinly
1 large green capsicum (350g), sliced thinly
1 large yellow capsicum (350g), sliced thinly
1 large red onion (300g), sliced thinly
16 small flour tortillas (16cm diameter)
3 cups finely shredded iceberg lettuce
1¼ cups (150g) coarsely grated low-fat cheddar cheese
fresh tomato salsa
3 medium tomatoes (450g), seeded, chopped finely
1 medium red onion (170g), chopped finely
1 tablespoon finely chopped drained
    jalapeño chillies, optional
¼ cup finely chopped fresh coriander
1 tablespoon lemon juice

method

1 Heat large oiled grill plate (or grill or barbecue). Cook beef until browned and cooked as desired. Cover; stand 10 minutes then slice thinly.
2 Meanwhile, cook capsicums and onion, in batches, on grill plate until vegetables are browned all over.
3 Heat tortillas according to manufacturer's instructions on package.
4 Meanwhile, make fresh tomato salsa.
5 Divide beef slices and vegetables among tortillas on serving plates; top with lettuce and cheese, roll to enclose filling. Serve with separate bowl of fresh tomato salsa.
    fresh tomato salsa Combine ingredients in small bowl.

Lamb kofta with yogurt and chilli tomato sauces

ingredients

1kg lean lamb mince
1 large brown onion (200g), chopped finely
1 clove garlic, crushed
1 tablespoon ground cumin
2 teaspoons ground turmeric
2 teaspoons ground allspice
1 tablespoon finely chopped fresh mint
2 tablespoons finely chopped fresh flat-leaf parsley
1 egg, beaten lightly
6 pocket pitta bread (510g), quartered
yogurt sauce
200g low-fat yogurt
1 clove garlic, crushed
1 tablespoon finely chopped fresh flat-leaf parsley
chilli tomato sauce
¼ cup (60ml) tomato sauce
¼ cup (60ml) chilli sauce

preparation time *15 minutes*
cooking time *20 minutes* serves *6*
nutritional count per serving
8.2g total fat (3.1g saturated fat);
1547kJ (370 cal); 28.1g carbohydrate;
43.9g protein; 2.5g fibre

method

1 Combine lamb, onion, garlic, spices, herbs and egg in large bowl; shape mixture into 18 balls.
2 Mould balls around 18 skewers to form sausage shapes. Cook, in batches, on heated oiled grill plate (or grill or barbecue) until browned all over and cooked through.
3 Meanwhile, make yogurt sauce; make chilli tomato sauce.
4 Serve kofta with pitta and sauces.
   yogurt sauce Combine ingredients in small bowl.
   chilli tomato sauce Combine ingredients in small bowl.

Soak 18 bamboo skewers in water
for at least an hour before using
to prevent them from scorching
and splintering during cooking.

Minty lamb cutlets with mixed vegie smash

ingredients

1 tablespoon finely chopped fresh mint
⅓ cup (110g) mint jelly
1 teaspoon finely grated lemon rind
2 teaspoons olive oil
8 french-trimmed lamb cutlets (400g)
mixed vegie smash
600g baby new potatoes, halved
2 large carrots (360g), cut into 2cm pieces
1 cup (120g) frozen peas
1 tablespoon olive oil
1 tablespoon lemon juice
2 tablespoons finely chopped fresh mint

method

1 Make mixed vegie smash.
2 Combine mint and jelly in small bowl.
3 Rub combined rind and oil over lamb; cook lamb
   on heated oiled grill plate (or grill or barbecue)
   until cooked as desired.
4 Serve lamb with smash and mint mixture.
   mixed vegie smash Boil, steam or microwave potato,
   carrot and peas, separately, until tender; drain. Crush
   potato and peas roughly in large bowl; stir in carrot
   and remaining ingredients.
   preparation time *10 minutes* cooking time *30 minutes*
   serves *4* nutritional count per serving *15.8g total fat*
   (4.9g saturated fat); 1572kJ (376 cal); 38.4g carbohydrate;
   16.3g protein; 7.3g fibre

ingredients

250g rice vermicelli noodles
4 eggs, beaten lightly
2 teaspoons vegetable oil
1 medium brown onion (150g), chopped coarsely
2 cloves garlic, crushed
2cm piece fresh ginger (10g), grated
150g baby buk choy, chopped coarsely
200g snow peas, halved
1 small red capsicum (150g), sliced thickly
2 tablespoons japanese soy sauce
2 tablespoons oyster sauce
2 tablespoons sweet chilli sauce
1 cup loosely packed fresh coriander leaves
3 cups (240g) bean sprouts

method

1 Place noodles in large heatproof bowl, cover with boiling water; stand until just tender, drain. Using scissors, cut noodles into 10cm lengths.
2 Heat lightly oiled wok; add half the egg, swirl wok to make thin omelette. Cook, uncovered, until egg is just set. Remove from wok; repeat with remaining egg. Roll tightly; cut into thin strips.
3 Heat oil in wok; stir-fry onion until soft. Add garlic and ginger; cook, stirring, 1 minute. Add buk choy, snow peas, capsicum and sauces; cook, stirring, until vegetables are just tender.
4 Add noodles and egg strips to wok with coriander and sprouts; toss gently to combine.
preparation time *15 minutes (plus standing time)*
cooking time *15 minutes* serves *4*
nutritional count per serving *8.3g total fat
(2g saturated fat); 1463kJ (350 cal);
51.6g carbohydrate; 12.5g protein; 7.6g fibre*

Singapore noodles

Pappardelle pasta is also known as lasagnette or mafalde, and is cut into flat, wide ribbons sometimes with scalloped edges. Tagliatelle, fettuccine or narrow lasagne can be substituted.

ingredients

4 medium tomatoes (600g), each cut into 8 wedges
¼ cup (60ml) balsamic vinegar
3 cloves garlic, crushed
375g pappardelle pasta
100g baby spinach leaves, trimmed
2 tablespoons olive oil
1 cup (240g) low-fat ricotta

method

1 Preheat oven to 200°C/180°C fan-forced.
2 Place tomato, in single layer, on oven tray; pour combined vinegar and garlic over tomato. Roast, uncovered, about 25 minutes or until tomato is browned lightly and softened.
3 Cook pasta in large saucepan of boiling water, uncovered, until just tender; drain.
4 Combine pasta, tomato, spinach and oil in large bowl. Break ricotta into small pieces; add to pasta mixture, toss gently.

preparation time *10 minutes* cooking time *25 minutes* serves *4* nutritional count per serving *14.8g total fat (4.3g saturated fat); 2057kJ (492 cal); 68.2g carbohydrate; 18g protein; 5.9g fibre*

Pappardelle with roasted tomato, spinach and ricotta

ingredients

8 lamb fillets (800g)
1 tablespoon ground cumin
1 tablespoon ground coriander
1 teaspoon ground cinnamon
¾ cup (210g) low-fat yogurt
1½ cups (300g) couscous
1½ cups (375ml) boiling water
1 teaspoon peanut oil
⅓ cup (55g) dried currants
2 teaspoons finely grated lemon rind
2 teaspoons lemon juice
¼ cup coarsely chopped fresh coriander

method

1 Combine lamb, spices and ⅓ cup of the yogurt in medium bowl, cover; refrigerate 3 hours or overnight.
2 Cook lamb on heated oiled grill plate (or grill or barbecue) until browned and cooked as desired. Cover; stand 5 minutes then slice thinly.
3 Meanwhile, combine couscous, water and oil in large heatproof bowl, cover; stand 5 minutes or until liquid is absorbed, fluffing with fork occasionally. Stir in currants, rind, juice and coriander leaves; toss with fork to combine.
4 Serve lamb with couscous; drizzle with remaining yogurt.

preparation time *15 minutes (plus refrigeration time)*
cooking time *15 minutes* serves *4*
nutritional count per serving *8.1g total fat (3.1g saturated fat); 2307kJ (552 cal); 68.8g carbohydrate; 49g protein; 1.6g fibre*

Moroccan lamb with couscous

You could substitute some finely chopped preserved lemon for the lemon juice and rind in the couscous.

Teriyaki lamb stir-fry

ingredients

2 teaspoons olive oil
800g lean lamb strips
2 teaspoons sesame oil
2 cloves garlic, crushed
1 medium brown onion (150g), sliced thickly
1 fresh long red chilli, seeded, sliced thinly
⅓ cup (80ml) teriyaki sauce
¼ cup (60ml) sweet chilli sauce
500g baby buk choy, quartered
175g broccolini, chopped coarsely

method

1 Heat olive oil in wok; stir-fry lamb, in batches, until cooked as desired.
2 Heat sesame oil in wok; stir-fry garlic, onion and chilli until fragrant. Add sauces; bring to the boil. Add buk choy and broccolini; stir-fry until buk choy just wilts and broccolini is just tender. Return lamb to wok; stir-fry until heated through.

preparation time *10 minutes* cooking time *20 minutes* serves *4* nutritional count per serving *12.6g total fat (3.9g saturated fat); 1463kJ (350 cal); 7.2g carbohydrate; 49.1g protein; 4.9g fibre*

Pesto fish kebabs

You can use any large fish fillets or steaks — such as ling, gemfish, snapper, kingfish or silver warehou — for this recipe.

Fish can be marinated and threaded onto skewers a day ahead; store, covered, in the refrigerator.

Soak eight bamboo skewers in water for at least an hour before using to prevent them from scorching and splintering during cooking.

serving suggestion
Serve with lemon-scented steamed rice.

ingredients
600g firm white fish fillets
1 tablespoon bottled pesto
½ cup finely chopped fresh flat-leaf parsley
½ small savoy cabbage (600g), shredded finely
⅓ cup (65g) rinsed, drained baby capers
1 teaspoon finely grated lemon rind
½ cup finely chopped fresh mint

method
1 Cut fish into 2cm cubes; combine with pesto and 1 tablespoon of the parsley in medium bowl. Thread onto eight skewers.
2 Cook kebabs, in batches, in heated large oiled frying pan until browned and cooked through. Cover to keep warm.
3 Add cabbage to heated pan; cook, stirring, until just tender. Stir in remaining parsley, capers, rind and mint.
4 Serve fish kebabs on stir-fried cabbage.
preparation time *10 minutes* cooking time *15 minutes* serves *4* nutritional count per serving *5.5g total fat (1.5g saturated fat); 920kJ (220 cal); 5.2g carbohydrate; 34g protein; 6.3g fibre*

Penne with tomato salsa and tuna

The Italian name of this pasta means "pen", a reference to the nib-like, pointy ends of each piece of pasta. Penne comes in both smooth (lisce) and ridged (rigate) versions, and in a variety of sizes. You can substitute any pasta for the penne in this recipe.

ingredients

375g penne
3 medium tomatoes (450g), seeded, chopped finely
1 medium red onion (170g), chopped finely
2 cloves garlic, crushed
¼ cup firmly packed, torn fresh basil leaves
425g can tuna in brine, drained, flaked
¼ cup (60ml) balsamic vinegar

method

1 Cook pasta in large saucepan of boiling water, uncovered, until just tender; drain.
2 Combine pasta with remaining ingredients in large bowl; toss gently.
preparation time *15 minutes* cooking time *10 minutes* serves *4* nutritional count per serving *3.5g total fat (1.1g saturated fat); 1927kJ (461 cal); 69.1g carbohydrate; 34g protein; 5.6g fibre*

serving suggestion
Serve with ciabatta bread and a mixed green salad.

ingredients

12 baby new potatoes (480g), halved
4 medium zucchini (480g), quartered lengthways
2 tablespoons olive oil
4 x 200g white fish fillets
2 medium egg tomatoes (150g), chopped finely
2 tablespoons lemon juice
1 tablespoon finely chopped fresh dill
2 tablespoons finely chopped fresh basil

method

1 Boil, steam or microwave potato and zucchini, separately, until tender; drain.
2 Meanwhile, heat half the oil in large frying pan; cook fish until cooked through. Remove from pan; cover to keep warm.
3 Heat remaining oil in cleaned pan; cook tomato and juice, stirring, 2 minutes. Remove from heat; stir in herbs.
4 Divide fish and vegetables among plates; drizzle with tomato mixture.

*preparation time 10 minutes cooking time 20 minutes
serves 4 nutritional count per serving 10.8g total fat
(1.5g saturated fat); 1371kJ (328 cal); 18.5g carbohydrate;
38.1g protein; 4.6g fibre*

Fish with herb and tomato dressing

We used blue-eye in this recipe, but you can use any firm white fish, such as perch or ling.

You could use any firm-fleshed white fish fillets for this recipe – we used blue-eye. Make the breadcrumbs from bread that is at least a day old; grate or process stale bread to make crumbs.

Cheese-crumbed fish fillets with stir-fried vegetables

ingredients

1 cup (70g) stale wholemeal
   breadcrumbs
½ cup (45g) rolled oats
1 tablespoon rinsed, drained
   capers, chopped finely
2 teaspoons finely grated
   lemon rind
¼ cup (20g) finely grated
   romano cheese
¼ cup finely chopped fresh
   flat-leaf parsley
1 tablespoon sesame oil
4 x 200g firm white fish fillets
½ cup (75g) plain flour
2 egg whites, beaten lightly
1 large carrot (180g), cut into
   thin strips
2 trimmed celery stalks (200g),
   cut into thin strips
1 medium green capsicum (200g),
   cut into thin strips
6 green onions, chopped finely
1 fresh small red thai chilli, seeded,
   chopped finely
1 tablespoon sesame seeds

method

1 Preheat oven to 220°C/200°C fan-forced.
2 Combine breadcrumbs, oats, capers, rind, cheese,
   parsley and oil in medium bowl.
3 Coat fish in flour, shake off excess; dip in egg white,
   then in breadcrumb mixture.
4 Place fish, in single layer, in baking dish; bake, uncovered,
   about 15 minutes or until cooked through.
5 Meanwhile, stir-fry carrot in heated wok. Add celery,
   capsicum, onion, chilli and sesame seeds; stir-fry until
   vegetables are just tender.
6 Serve sliced fish on stir-fried vegetables.
   preparation time *15 minutes* cooking time *15 minutes*
   serves *4* nutritional count per serving *12.7g total fat*
   (3g saturated fat); 1751kJ (419 cal); 31.9g carbohydrate;
   41g protein; 5.6g fibre

Fish can be crumbed
several hours ahead;
store, covered, in
the refrigerator.

serving suggestion
Serve with wedges
of lime or lemon.

5.
Something sweet

Orange crème caramels

ingredients

1¼ cups (275g) caster sugar
½ cup (125ml) water
¼ cup (60ml) orange juice
2 cups (500ml) low-fat milk
3 eggs
3 egg yolks
1 teaspoon vanilla extract
2 teaspoons finely grated orange rind

method

1 Preheat oven to 160°C/140°C fan-forced.
2 Combine ¾ cup of the sugar with the water in medium heavy-based saucepan; stir over low heat, without boiling, until sugar dissolves. Bring to the boil; boil, uncovered, without stirring, until mixture is caramel in colour. Remove from heat; add juice (some of the toffee will set; stir over low heat until toffee melts). Divide mixture among six ½-cup (125ml) ovenproof dishes.
3 Bring milk to the boil in small saucepan. Whisk remaining sugar, eggs, egg yolks and extract in medium bowl; whisk hot milk gradually into egg mixture. Stir in the rind; pour mixture over toffee in dishes.
4 Place dishes in medium baking dish; add enough boiling water to come halfway up the sides of dishes. Bake about 45 minutes or until custards set. Remove dishes from baking dish; cool 10 minutes. Cover; refrigerate overnight.
5 Use fingers to gently ease custard away from the side of the dish, then invert onto individual serving plates.

preparation time *20 minutes (plus refrigeration time)*
cooking time *1 hour* serves *6*
nutritional count per serving *3.8g total fat
(1.8g saturated fat); 1170kJ (280 cal);
52.8g carbohydrate; 7.9g protein; 0.1g fibre*

Soak eight 20cm-long wooden skewers in
water for an hour before using to prevent
them splintering or scorching during cooking.

You need half a medium-sized pineapple (625g) for this recipe.

*Tropical fruit skewers with orange glaze

ingredients

1 teaspoon finely grated orange rind
¼ cup (60ml) orange juice
2 tablespoons brown sugar
2 medium bananas (400g)
250g strawberries
600g piece pineapple
1 starfruit (160g)
200g low-fat vanilla yogurt

method

1 Combine rind, juice and sugar in small saucepan; stir over low heat until sugar dissolves. Cool.
2 Preheat grill.
3 Peel bananas; slice thickly crossways. Hull and halve strawberries. Peel pineapple; cut into chunks. Slice starfruit thickly.
4 Thread fruits, alternately, onto skewers. Place skewers on oven tray lined with baking paper; pour orange mixture over skewers.
5 Grill skewers, turning occasionally, about 10 minutes or until browned lightly. Serve with yogurt.
preparation time *20 minutes* cooking time *15 minutes* serves *4* nutritional count per serving *0.5g total fat (0.1g saturated fat); 974kJ (233 cal); 45.9g carbohydrate; 7.1g protein; 7.3g fibre*

1. Watermelon and strawberry ice-block

Combine ⅓ cup water and 2 tablespoons white sugar in a small saucepan; stir over low heat until sugar dissolves. Bring to the boil; boil, uncovered, about 2 minutes or until mixture thickens slightly. Transfer syrup to small bowl; refrigerate until cold. Blend or process cold syrup with 250g peeled, seeded and coarsely chopped watermelon, 80g hulled and coarsely chopped strawberries and 2 teaspoons lemon juice until smooth. Pour mixture into four ⅓-cup (80ml) ice-block moulds. Freeze overnight or until firm.

preparation time *10 minutes (plus refrigeration and freezing time)* cooking time *5 minutes* makes *4* nutritional count per ice-block *0.2g total fat (0g saturated fat); 238kJ (57 cal); 12.7g carbohydrate; 0.5g protein; 0.8g fibre*

2. ✳ Lemonade, lemon and mint ice-block

Combine 1½ cups lemonade, 1 teaspoon finely grated lemon rind, 1 tablespoon lemon juice and 2 teaspoons finely chopped fresh mint in medium freezer-proof jug; freeze mixture about 1 hour or until partially frozen. Stir; pour into four ⅓-cup (80ml) ice-block moulds. Freeze overnight until firm.

preparation time *5 minutes (plus freezing time)* makes *4* nutritional count per ice-block *0g total fat (0g saturated fat); 176kJ (42 cal); 10.3g carbohydrate; 0.1g protein; 0g fibre*

3. ✳ Honey, banana and yogurt ice-block

Blend or process 1 large coarsely chopped banana, ⅔ cup vanilla yogurt and 1 tablespoon honey until smooth and creamy. Pour into four ⅓-cup (80ml) ice-block moulds. Freeze overnight until firm.

preparation time *5 minutes (plus freezing time)* makes *4* nutritional count per ice-block *1.7g total fat (1.1g saturated fat); 435kJ (104 cal); 18.4g carbohydrate; 3.1g protein; 0.8g fibre*

4. ✳ Frozen fruit and yogurt blocks

Combine 1½ cups vanilla yogurt, 1 cup frozen mixed berries and 1 tablespoon honey in medium bowl; spoon into six ¼-cup (60ml) ice-block moulds. Press lids on firmly; freeze overnight until firm.

preparation time *5 minutes (plus freezing time)* makes *6* nutritional count per ice-block *2.4g total fat (1.5g saturated fat); 380kJ (91 cal); 12.5g carbohydrate; 3.8g protein; 1g fibre*

1

3

2

4

137

Frozen green apple yogurt

Refreshing frozen yogurt certainly gives ice-cream a run for its money.

ingredients

⅓ cup (115g) honey
½ cup (125ml) apple juice
1 teaspoon gelatine
¾ cup (130g) finely grated unpeeled apple
500g greek-style yogurt
1 tablespoon passionfruit pulp

method

1 Stir honey and juice in small saucepan over low heat until honey melts; cool syrup 5 minutes. Sprinkle gelatine over syrup; stir until gelatine dissolves.
2 Combine gelatine mixture, apple and yogurt in 14cm x 21cm loaf pan. Cover with foil; freeze 3 hours or overnight. Remove yogurt from freezer about 15 minutes before serving. Top yogurts with passionfruit pulp.

preparation time *15 minutes (plus freezing time)*
cooking time *5 minutes* serves *4*
nutritional count per serving *4.3g total fat (2.8g saturated fat); 932kJ (223 cal); 37.4g carbohydrate; 7g protein; 2g fibre*

variations

raspberry Substitute water for the apple juice in syrup; substitute 150g thawed frozen raspberries for the apple. Push thawed raspberries through a fine sieve over small bowl; discard seeds. Combine raspberry puree with gelatine mixture and yogurt and continue as per step 2.
nutritional count per serving
4.4g total fat (2.8g saturated fat); 840kJ (201 cal); 31.7g carbohydrate; 7.1g protein; 2g fibre

mango Substitute water for the apple juice in syrup; substitute 300g thawed coarsely chopped frozen mango for the apple. Combine mango with gelatine mixture and yogurt and continue as per step 2.
nutritional count per serving
4.4g total fat (2.8g saturated fat); 957kJ (229 cal); 38.9g carbohydrate; 4.4g protein; 1.1g fibre

You need to buy an apple weighing about 275g for this recipe.

Upside-down cake with caramelised apple

preparation time *15 minutes*
cooking time *25 minutes* serves *8*
nutritional count per serving
10g total fat (5.8g saturated fat);
970kJ (232 cal); 28.9g carbohydrate;
4.9g protein; 1.7g fibre

ingredients

2 large apples (400g)
60g unsalted butter, chopped
½ cup (110g) firmly packed brown sugar
1 teaspoon ground cinnamon
⅓ cup (50g) wholemeal self-raising flour
⅓ cup (80ml) low-fat milk
4 eggs, separated
¼ cup (55g) caster sugar
2 tablespoons flaked coconut

method

1 Preheat oven to 200°C/180°C fan-forced.
2 Peel and core apples; slice into 5mm rings.
3 Melt butter in heavy-based 25cm frying pan; add brown sugar and cinnamon. Cook, stirring, until sugar dissolves. Remove from heat.
4 Place apple rings, overlapping slightly, on top of caramel in pan. Return to heat; cook, covered, over low heat, 2 minutes. Uncover; cook, over low heat, about 5 minutes or until apples are tender. Remove from heat.
5 Meanwhile, combine flour, milk and egg yolks in medium bowl.
6 Beat egg whites in small bowl with electric mixer until soft peaks form; gradually add caster sugar, beating until dissolved between additions. Fold egg white mixture into flour mixture, in two batches.
7 Spread mixture carefully over apple in pan. Bake, uncovered, in oven, about 12 minutes.
8 Turn onto serving plate; serve sprinkled with coconut and, if you like, vanilla ice-cream.

Berry-muesli baked apples

ingredients

4 large granny smith apples (800g)
cooking-oil spray
⅓ cup (35g) natural muesli
½ cup (75g) fresh blueberries
20g butter, melted
3 teaspoons brown sugar

method

1 Preheat oven to 160°C/140°C fan-forced.
2 Core unpeeled apples about three-quarters of the way
   down from stem end, making hole 4cm in diameter. Use
   small sharp knife to score around centre of each apple;
   lightly spray with cooking oil.
3 Combine remaining ingredients in small bowl. Divide
   mixture among apples, pressing firmly into holes; place
   apples in small baking dish. Bake, uncovered, about
   45 minutes or until apples are just softened.
   preparation time *25 minutes* cooking time *45 minutes*
   serves *4* nutritional count per serving *5.4g total fat
   (2.9g saturated fat); 681kJ (163 cal); 26g carbohydrate;
   1.4g protein; 4.4g fibre*

ingredients

12 (140g) savoiardi sponge finger biscuits
1 cup (250ml) cranberry juice
400g low-fat french vanilla frûche
150g fresh raspberries
150g fresh blueberries

method

1 Dip biscuits in juice; divide among four 1½-cup (375ml) serving glasses. Sprinkle remaining juice over biscuits.
2 Divide half the frûche mixture among glasses; sprinkle with half the combined berries. Repeat layering with remaining frûche and remaining berries.
preparation time *15 minutes* serves *4*
nutritional count per serving *2.1g total fat (0.7g saturated fat); 1095kJ (262 cal); 47g carbohydrate; 11.9g protein; 3.1g fibre*

✳ Mixed berries with sponge fingers

You need to buy three passionfruits for this recipe.

preparation time *25 minutes (plus refrigeration time)* serves *8* nutritional count per serving *7.1g total fat (4.2g saturated fat); 1129kJ (270 cal); 46.4g carbohydrate; 8.7g protein; 4.5g fibre*

ingredients

85g packet raspberry jelly crystals
1 cup (135g) fresh or frozen raspberries
6 x 30g jam rollettes, sliced thickly
250g strawberries, quartered
1 small orange (180g), segmented
2 medium kiwifruits (170g), peeled, chopped coarsely
¼ cup (60ml) passionfruit pulp
250g reduced-fat cream cheese, softened
1 tablespoon icing sugar
1½ cups (420g) low-fat mixed berry yogurt
1 starfruit (160g), cut into 8 slices

method

1 Make jelly according to directions on packet; divide among eight 1-cup (250ml) serving glasses, sprinkle with raspberries. Cover; refrigerate 3 hours or until jelly is firm.
2 Top jelly with rollette slices then strawberries, orange, kiwifruit and passionfruit pulp.
3 Beat cream cheese and icing sugar in small bowl with electric mixer until smooth. Gradually beat in yogurt; spread mixture over fruit in glasses. Cover trifles; refrigerate 1 hour. Top with starfruit to serve.

Fruit salad and yogurt trifle

The goodness of fruit salad combined with jam rollettes and jelly bring a special touch to this scrummy layered dessert. Jam rollettes (also known as mini swiss rolls) are available in most supermarkets.

Fruit salad with star-anise syrup

You can make the syrup up to two days ahead and refrigerate, covered, until ready to use. Reheat before pouring over the fruit, as described in step 3.

You can use this syrup with any fruit, for instance, a selection of tropical varieties such as carambola, rambutan, pineapple, mango or mangosteen.

serving suggestion
For an extra special grand finale, dollop with mascarpone.

ingredients
1 small honeydew melon (1.3kg)
250g strawberries
400g cherries
4 cardamom pods
4 star anise
½ cup (110g) caster sugar
¼ cup (60ml) lemon juice
¼ cup (60ml) water

method
1 Halve, peel and chop melon coarsely. Cut strawberries in half. Seed cherries; place fruit in large bowl.
2 Bruise cardamom pods; place in small saucepan with star anise, sugar, juice and the water. Stir over heat, without boiling, until sugar dissolves.
3 Pour warm syrup over fruit; refrigerate, covered, about 30 minutes or until cold.
preparation time *30 minutes (plus refrigeration time)*
cooking time *5 minutes* serves *4*
nutritional count per serving *0.8g total fat
(0g saturated fat); 974kJ (233 cal);
50.2g carbohydrate; 3.3g protein; 4.7g fibre*

Top Tip

Use the terms 'everyday' and 'sometime' foods, rather than 'bad' and 'good' foods. There is a place for all food in a healthy diet – frequency and quantity are the things to watch out for.

Pavlova roll with banana, kiwi and passionfruit

ingredients

4 egg whites
¾ cup (165g) caster sugar
1 teaspoon cornflour
1 teaspoon white vinegar
1 teaspoon vanilla extract
1 tablespoon icing sugar
300ml thickened light cream
1 large banana (230g), halved lengthways, sliced thinly
2 medium kiwifruit (170g), quartered lengthways
⅓ cup (80ml) passionfruit pulp

method

1 Preheat oven to 160°C/140°C fan-forced. Grease 25cm x 30cm swiss roll pan; line base with baking paper, extending paper 5cm over long sides.
2 Beat egg whites in small bowl with electric mixer until soft peaks form. Gradually add caster sugar, 1 tablespoon at a time, beating until sugar dissolves between additions. Fold in cornflour, vinegar and extract. Spread meringue mixture into pan; bake, uncovered, about 20 minutes or until browned lightly.
3 Turn meringue onto sheet of baking paper sprinkled with half the sifted icing sugar; remove lining paper, trim short ends of meringue.
4 Beat cream and remaining sifted icing sugar in small bowl with electric mixer until soft peaks form. Spread cream mixture over slightly warm meringue; place fruit lengthways along centre of meringue, spoon pulp over fruit. Roll meringue firmly from long side, using paper as a guide. Refrigerate until ready to serve.

preparation time *25 minutes*
cooking time *20 minutes*
serves *10*
nutritional count per serving
8.1g total fat
(5.3g saturated fat);
748kJ (179 cal);
24.6g carbohydrate;
3g protein; 1.9g fibre

You need to buy four passionfruit to get the amount of pulp needed for this recipe.

ingredients

½ cup (100g) white short-grain rice
2 cups (500ml) milk
1 cup (250ml) skim milk
1 teaspoon vanilla extract
¼ cup (55g) caster sugar
raspberry compote
300g frozen raspberries
1 tablespoon caster sugar

method

1 Preheat oven to 160°C/140°C fan-forced.
2 Rinse rice well under cold water; drain. Spread rice over bottom of shallow 1-litre (4-cup) baking dish.
3 Combine milks, extract and sugar in medium saucepan; bring to the boil. Pour hot milk mixture carefully over rice in baking dish; mix gently with fork. Cover dish tightly with foil; bake about 1¼ hours or until rice is softened and almost all liquid is absorbed.
4 Meanwhile, make raspberry compote.
5 Serve compote with pudding.
   raspberry compote Combine ingredients in small saucepan; stir over low heat until sugar dissolves. Cool 10 minutes.

preparation time *10 minutes*
cooking time *1 hour 20 minutes* serves *4*
nutritional count per serving *5.4g total fat (3.3g saturated fat); 1237kJ (296 cal); 52.1g carbohydrate; 9.6g protein; 4.3g fibre*

Rice pudding with raspberries

Apple berry crumbles

ingredients

2 medium apples (300g)
¾ cup (115g) frozen mixed berries
2 tablespoons lemon juice
2 tablespoons brown sugar
2 tablespoons plain flour
¼ cup (20g) rolled oats
20g butter
¼ cup (30g) finely chopped roasted hazelnuts

method

1 Preheat oven to 200°C/180°C fan-forced. Grease four ¾-cup (180ml) ovenproof dishes; place on oven tray.
2 Peel and core apples; chop coarsely. Combine apple, berries, juice and half the sugar in medium bowl; divide mixture among dishes.
3 Combine remaining sugar, flour and oats in small bowl. Rub butter into flour mixture; stir in nuts. Divide crumble over fruit mixture, pressing down firmly. Bake, uncovered, about 30 minutes or until browned lightly.
4 Serve crumbles dusted with sifted icing sugar and accompanied with yogurt, if you like.
preparation time *15 minutes* cooking time *30 minutes* serves *4* nutritional count per serving *9.3g total fat (3g saturated fat); 803kJ (192 cal); 22.3g carbohydrate; 3.1g protein; 3.1g fibre*

Warm raspberry meringue pots

ingredients

2 cups (300g) frozen raspberries
2 tablespoons caster sugar
1 teaspoon cornflour
1 tablespoon orange juice
3 egg whites
¾ cup (165g) caster sugar, extra
2 teaspoons cornflour, extra
2 teaspoons white vinegar

preparation time *20 minutes*
cooking time *45 minutes* serves *4*
nutritional count per serving
0.3g total fat (0g saturated fat);
1024kJ (245 cal); 56.3g carbohydrate;
3.6g protein; 4.1g fibre

method

1 Preheat oven to 160°C/140°C fan-forced.
2 Combine berries and sugar in small saucepan; stir over low heat until sugar dissolves. Stir in blended cornflour and juice; cook, stirring, until mixture boils and thickens slightly.
3 Process half the berry mixture until smooth. Place in medium bowl then stir in unprocessed berry mixture; divide among four 1-cup (250ml) ovenproof dishes.
4 Beat egg whites in small bowl with electric mixer until soft peaks form. Gradually add extra sugar, beating until sugar dissolves between additions; fold in sifted extra cornflour and the vinegar.
5 Spoon meringue over berry mixture in dishes; bake, uncovered, about 30 minutes or until meringue is browned lightly.

Wipe the outsides of panna cotta moulds with a hot cloth to make turning them out onto serving plates easier.

Vanilla panna cotta with berry compote

ingredients

2 tablespoons boiling water
2 tablespoons honey
1 vanilla bean
2 teaspoons gelatine
1½ cups (420g) yogurt
berry compote
2 cups (300g) frozen mixed berries
¼ cup (40g) icing sugar

preparation time *15 minutes*
(plus refrigeration time)
cooking time *10 minutes* serves *4*
nutritional count per serving
3.7g total fat (2.3g saturated fat);
844kJ (202 cal); 32.8g carbohydrate;
7.1g protein; 3.3g fibre

method

1 Combine the water and honey in small heatproof jug. Split vanilla bean in half lengthways; scrape seeds into jug then place pod in jug. Sprinkle gelatine over honey mixture; stand jug in small saucepan of simmering water. Stir until gelatine dissolves; cool 5 minutes. Discard vanilla pod.
2 Combine honey mixture and yogurt in small bowl; stir until smooth. Strain into four ½-cup (125ml) moulds, cover; refrigerate 3 hours or overnight.
3 Make berry compote.
4 Turn panna cotta onto serving plates; serve with berry compote.
   berry compote Combine ingredients in medium saucepan over low heat, uncovered, stirring occasionally, about 5 minutes or until berries just soften. Transfer to small bowl; cool 10 minutes. Cover; refrigerate until required.

A galette is a French flaky pastry tart that can be either savoury or sweet, and makes a popular summer dessert. Any of the season's stone fruits, such as plums or nectarines, can be substituted for the peaches.

*Peach galette

ingredients

1 sheet ready-rolled puff pastry with canola, thawed
3 medium peaches (450g)
1 tablespoon brown sugar
1 tablespoon plum jam, warmed, strained

preparation time *10 minutes*
cooking time *15 minutes* serves *6*
nutritional count per serving
6.4g total fat (0.5g saturated fat);
589kJ (141 cal); 18.2g carbohydrate;
2.1g protein; 1.3g fibre

method

1 Preheat oven to 220°C/200°C fan-forced. Grease oven tray.
2 Place pastry sheet on tray.
3 Place unpeeled peaches in large heatproof bowl; cover with boiling water. Stand about 1 minute or until skins can be slipped off easily. Slice peaches thinly; discard seeds.
4 Arrange peach slices on pastry, leaving 2cm border around edge; fold over edges of pastry. Sprinkle sugar evenly over peach galette.
5 Bake, uncovered, about 15 minutes or until pastry is browned lightly. Brush hot galette with jam. Serve dusted with sifted icing sugar, if desired.

Maple syrup is the processed sap of
the maple tree. Maple-flavoured syrup
or pancake syrup, is made from cane
sugar and artificial maple flavouring,
and is not an adequate substitute.

Apple and cinnamon pancakes with maple syrup

ingredients

1 cup (150g) self-raising flour
¼ cup (55g) firmly packed
    brown sugar
½ teaspoon ground cinnamon
½ cup (125ml) skim milk
1 egg yolk
½ cup (110g) canned pie apple,
    chopped coarsely
2 egg whites
2 granny smith apples (300g)
2 tablespoons brown sugar, extra
200g low-fat vanilla ice-cream
2 tablespoons pure maple syrup

preparation time *20 minutes*
cooking time *20 minutes* serves *4*
nutritional count per serving
3.6g total fat (1.5g saturated fat);
1630kJ (390 cal); 76.6g carbohydrate;
10g protein; 3.3g fibre

method

1 Combine flour in large bowl with sugar, cinnamon, milk, egg yolk and canned pie apple.
2 Beat egg whites in small bowl with electric mixer until soft peaks form; fold gently into apple mixture.
3 Heat medium oiled frying pan; pour ¼-cup amounts of batter for each pancake into pan. Cook until browned both sides; repeat with remaining batter. You will have eight pancakes.
4 Meanwhile, peel and core apples; cut into wedges. Cook apple and extra sugar over low heat in same pan, stirring, until apple caramelises.
5 Divide pancakes among serving dishes. Top with apple mixture then ice-cream; drizzle with maple syrup.
serving suggestion A flavoured ice-cream, such as toffee crunch or butterscotch, can be used instead of plain vanilla; omit the maple syrup if you use a flavoured ice-cream.

6.
Baking day

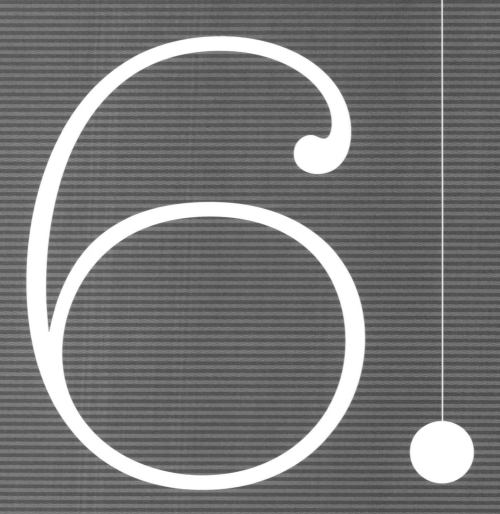

You can use milk or dark chocolate instead of white for the muffins and you'll still get the same melt-in-the-mouth result. These muffins are best served warm.

ingredients

1½ cups (225g) wholemeal self-raising flour
½ cup (110g) caster sugar
2 tablespoons vegetable oil
2 eggs, beaten lightly
1 cup (280g) low-fat yogurt
1 cup (150g) frozen mixed berries
100g white eating chocolate, chopped coarsely

method

1 Preheat oven to 180°C/160°C fan-forced. Grease 12-hole (⅓-cup/80ml) muffin pan.
2 Combine flour and sugar in large bowl. Add remaining ingredients; mix batter until just combined. Divide batter among pan holes. Bake about 30 minutes.
3 Stand muffins 5 minutes before serving, dusted with sifted icing sugar, if you like.

preparation time *10 minutes* cooking time *25 minutes* makes *12* nutritional count per muffin *7.2g total fat (2.5g saturated fat); 807kJ (193 cal); 25.3g carbohydrate; 5.6g protein; 2.4g fibre*

*Yogurt, berry and white chocolate muffins

*Banana muffins with crunchy topping

ingredients

1¾ cups (260g) wholemeal self-raising flour
¾ cup (165g) firmly packed brown sugar
1 cup mashed banana
1 egg, beaten lightly
1 cup (250ml) buttermilk
¼ cup (60ml) vegetable oil
crunchy oat topping
1 cup (90g) rolled oats
½ teaspoon ground nutmeg
2 tablespoons honey

method

1 Preheat oven to 200°C/180°C fan-forced. Grease
   12-hole (⅓-cup/80ml) muffin pan.
2 Make crunchy oat topping.
3 Sift flour and sugar into large bowl; stir in banana,
   egg, buttermilk and oil. Divide mixture among pan
   holes; sprinkle with topping. Bake, uncovered, about
   20 minutes.
4 Stand muffins in pan 5 minutes; turn, top-side up, onto
   wire rack to cool.
   crunchy oat topping Blend or process oats until
   coarsely chopped. Combine oats, nutmeg and honey
   in small bowl.
   preparation time *20 minutes* cooking time *20 minutes*
   makes *12* nutritional count per serving *6.6g total fat
   (1.2g saturated fat); 966kJ (231 cal); 35.7g carbohydrate;
   5.3g protein; 3.4g fibre*

ingredients

425g can apricot halves
2¼ cups (335g) self-raising flour
¾ cup (165g) firmly packed brown sugar
1 egg
⅔ cup (160ml) buttermilk
½ cup (125ml) vegetable oil
⅓ cup (110g) apricot jam
coconut topping
¼ cup (35g) plain flour
1 tablespoon caster sugar
⅓ cup (25g) shredded coconut
30g butter

method

1 Preheat oven to 180°C/160°C fan-forced. Grease
  12-hole (⅓-cup/80ml) muffin pan.
2 Drain apricots, discard syrup; chop apricots coarsely.
3 Make coconut topping.
4 Combine flour and sugar in large bowl; use a fork
  to stir in apricot, then combined egg, buttermilk, oil
  and jam. Mixture should look lumpy, do not overmix.
5 Divide mixture among pan holes; sprinkle coconut
  topping over muffin mixture. Bake, uncovered,
  about 25 minutes.
6 Stand muffins in pan 5 minutes; turn, top-side up,
  onto wire rack to cool.
  coconut topping Combine flour, sugar and
  coconut in small bowl; rub butter into flour mixture.

✳Apricot and coconut muffins

preparation time *30 minutes*
cooking time *25 minutes* makes *12*
nutritional count per serving *14.1g total fat
(4.1g saturated fat); 1384kJ (331 cal);
45.3g carbohydrate; 4.6g protein; 2g fibre*

167

Strawberry jelly cakes

You need two large passionfruits for this recipe.

Jelly cakes will keep, stored in an airtight container in the refrigerator, for up to one week.

ingredients

125g butter, softened
½ teaspoon vanilla extract
½ cup (110g) caster sugar
2 eggs
1½ cups (225g) self-raising flour
⅓ cup (80ml) low-fat milk
1¾ cups (430ml) boiling water
85g packet strawberry jelly crystals
2 tablespoons passionfruit pulp
3 cups (225g) shredded coconut

preparation time 45 minutes (plus refrigeration time) cooking time 25 minutes makes 36 nutritional count per cake 6.7g total fat (5g saturated fat); 456kJ (109 cal); 10.2g carbohydrate; 1g protein; 1.2g fibre

method

1 Preheat oven to 180°C/160°C fan-forced. Grease deep 23cm-square cake pan; line base with baking paper.
2 Beat butter, extract and sugar in small bowl with electric mixer until light and fluffy. Add eggs, one at a time; beat until just combined. Stir in flour and milk until smooth; spread mixture into pan.
3 Bake about 25 minutes. Stand 5 minutes; turn, top-side up, onto wire rack to cool.
4 Meanwhile, stir the water and jelly in medium heatproof jug until crystals dissolve; stir pulp into jelly. Pour into 19cm x 29cm slice pan; refrigerate, stirring occasionally, until set to the consistency of unbeaten egg white.
5 Cut cake into 36 squares; dip each square into jelly then toss in coconut. Stand jelly cakes on tray; cover, refrigerate 30 minutes.

Date and apple muesli slice

ingredients

2 medium apples (300g), grated coarsely
2 tablespoons lemon juice
¼ cup (60ml) water
50g butter
2 cups (280g) seeded dates
2 cups (220g) natural muesli
1 cup (220g) firmly packed brown sugar
1 cup (150g) plain flour
1 teaspoon ground cinnamon

method

1 Preheat oven to 180°C/160°C fan-forced. Grease 25cm x 30cm swiss roll pan.
2 Combine apple, juice, the water, butter and dates in medium saucepan; bring to the boil. Reduce heat; simmer, covered, about 5 minutes or until apple is soft. Uncover; cook, stirring occasionally, about 5 minutes or until mixture thickens to a paste-like consistency.
3 Meanwhile, place muesli in large frying pan; stir over low heat about 5 minutes or until browned lightly. Combine muesli in large bowl with sugar, flour and cinnamon. Stir in date mixture.
4 Spread slice mixture into pan; bake, uncovered, in oven about 20 minutes or until firm. Cool in pan before cutting.
preparation time *15 minutes* cooking time *35 minutes* makes *32* nutritional count per slice *1.9g total fat (1g saturated fat); 456kJ (109 cal); 20.4g carbohydrate; 1.4g protein; 2.1g fibre*

ingredients

2 cups (300g) self-raising flour
¼ teaspoon ground cinnamon
90g cold butter, chopped
⅓ cup (75g) caster sugar
½ cup (80g) dried currants
½ cup (75g) dried apricots, chopped coarsely
½ cup (65g) dried cranberries
1 egg, beaten lightly
½ cup (125ml) milk, approximately
1 tablespoon raw sugar

method

1 Preheat oven to 200°C/180°C fan-forced. Grease two oven trays.
2 Combine flour and cinnamon in large bowl; rub in butter. Stir in caster sugar, fruit, egg and enough milk to give a moist but firm consistency.
3 Drop rounded tablespoons of mixture about 5cm apart on trays; sprinkle with raw sugar. Bake, uncovered, about 15 minutes or until browned lightly. Loosen cakes; cool on trays.

preparation time *15 minutes* cooking time *15 minutes* makes *20* nutritional count per cake *4.2g total fat (2.6g saturated fat) 564kJ (135 cal) 22.4g carbohydrate 2.4g protein 1.3g fibre*

✳ Cranberry, apricot and currant rock cakes

*Blueberry scones with vanilla frûche

ingredients
2 cups (300g) self-raising flour
2 tablespoons icing sugar
1¼ cups (310ml) buttermilk, approximately
150g blueberries
200g French Vanilla Frûche Lite

method
1 Preheat oven to 220°C/200°C fan-forced. Grease shallow 20cm-round sandwich pan.
2 Sift flour and icing sugar into large bowl; pour in enough buttermilk to mix to a sticky dough. Fold in blueberries.
3 Gently knead dough on lightly floured surface until smooth; flatten out dough to about a 3cm thickness. Using 5.5cm cutter, cut eight rounds from dough; place rounds, slightly touching, in pan. Bake, uncovered, about 20 minutes or until browned lightly; turn scones onto wire rack. Serve with frûche.
preparation time *10 minutes* cooking time *20 minutes* makes *8* nutritional count per scone *2.6g total fat (1.5g saturated fat) 832kJ (199 cal) 36.2g carbohydrate 7.1g protein 1.8g fibre*

cook's info
To prevent dough from sticking, dust the inside of the cutter with flour.

Home-baked treats are healthier and more tasty than store-bought ones, and the kids can be involved in their making.

Banana loaf

You need to mash one large overripe banana (230g) for this recipe.

ingredients

¾ cup (110g) wholemeal self-raising flour
½ cup (75g) self-raising flour
1 teaspoon ground cinnamon
20g butter
½ cup (110g) firmly packed brown sugar
1 egg
¼ cup (60ml) low-fat milk
½ cup mashed banana
⅓ cup (120g) honey
2 small bananas (260g), sliced thickly

method

1 Preheat oven to 200°C/180°C fan-forced. Grease 8cm x 26cm bar cake pan; line base with baking paper.
2 Process flours, cinnamon and butter until crumbly. Add sugar, egg, milk and mashed banana; pulse until ingredients are just combined. Pour mixture into pan.
3 Bake about 40 minutes. Stand loaf 5 minutes; turn, top-side up, onto wire rack to cool. Serve sliced, topped with honey and sliced banana.
preparation time *10 minutes* cooking time *40 minutes* serves *12* nutritional count per serving *2.1g total fat (1.1g saturated fat); 694kJ (166 cal); 32.4g carbohydrate; 3g protein; 1.8g fibre*

ingredients

125g butter, softened
1 teaspoon finely grated lemon rind
1 cup (220g) firmly packed brown sugar
1 egg yolk
⅓ cup mashed banana
1½ cups (225g) plain flour
½ teaspoon bicarbonate of soda
1 cup (90g) rolled oats
½ cup (75g) finely chopped dried dates
⅔ cup (60g) rolled oats, extra
4 dried dates (35g), seeded, chopped coarsely

method

1 Preheat oven to 180°C/160°C fan-forced. Grease oven trays; line with baking paper.
2 Beat butter, rind, sugar and egg yolk in small bowl with electric mixer until combined; stir in banana then sifted flour and soda, oats and dates.
3 Roll level tablespoons of mixture into balls; roll each ball in extra oats then place on trays 5cm apart. Press a piece of coarsely chopped date into centre of each ball. Bake about 15 minutes. Cool cookies on trays.
preparation time *20 minutes* cooking time *15 minutes* makes *28* nutritional count per cookie *4.4g total fat (2.6g saturated fat); 539kJ (129 cal); 19.9g carbohydrate; 1.7g protein; 1.7g fibre*

Banana, date and rolled oat cookies

You need one large overripe banana (230g) for this recipe.

Caramel banana pinwheels

ingredients

½ cup (110g) firmly packed brown sugar
1 cup (150g) self-raising flour
1 cup (160g) wholemeal self-raising flour
30g butter
3 small ripe bananas (390g)
½ cup (125ml) low-fat milk
⅓ cup (40g) finely chopped walnuts

method

1 Preheat oven to 200°C/180°C fan-forced. Grease 20cm-round sandwich pan; sprinkle base of pan with 2 tablespoons of the sugar.
2 Place flours and 1 tablespoon of the remaining sugar in medium bowl; rub in butter. Mash 1 banana, add to bowl with milk; mix to a soft, sticky dough. Knead dough on floured surface; roll dough to 30cm x 40cm shape.
3 Chop remaining bananas finely. Sprinkle remaining sugar over dough, top with nuts and extra banana.
4 Starting from long side, roll dough tightly; trim ends. Cut roll into 10 slices; place pinwheels, cut-side up, in single layer, in pan. Bake 30 minutes. Serve pinwheels warm.
preparation time *20 minutes* cooking time *30 minutes* makes *10* nutritional count per pinwheel *4.5g total fat (1.6g saturated fat); 786kJ (188 cal); 31g carbohydrate; 4.2g protein; 2.6g fibre*

Glossary

ALL-BRAN low-fat, high-fibre breakfast cereal based on wheat bran.

ALLSPICE also known as pimento or jamaican pepper; so-named because it tastes like a combination of nutmeg, cumin, clove and cinnamon – all spices.

BABY BUK CHOY also known as pak kat farang, shanghai bok choy, chinese chard or white cabbage; has a fresh, mild mustard taste.

BASIL an aromatic herb; there are many types, but the most commonly used is sweet basil.

BEANS
borlotti also known as roman beans or pink beans; interchangeable with pinto beans because both are pale pink or beige with dark red streaks.
kidney medium-size red bean, slightly floury in texture yet sweet in flavour.
refried pinto or borlotti beans, cooked twice-soaked and boiled, then mashed and fried.
white a generic term we use for canned or dried cannellini, great northern, navy or haricot beans.

BICARBONATE OF SODA also known as baking or carb soda.

BREAD
ciabatta in Italian, the word means slipper, which is the traditional shape of this white bread with a crisp crust.
french stick also known as french loaf, french bread or baguette; a long, narrow cylindrical loaf with a crisp brown crust and light chewy interior.
lavash flat, unleavened bread of Mediterranean origin.
pitta also known as lebanese bread. A wheat-flour pocket bread that separates easily into two thin rounds.
tortillas thin, round unleavened bread originating in Mexico. Made from either wheat flour or corn.
turkish also known as pide; comes in long (about 45cm) flat loaves as well as individual rounds (rolls).

BREADCRUMBS
fresh bread, usually white, processed into crumbs; good for stuffings and as a thickening agent.
packaged fine-textured, crunchy, purchased white breadcrumbs.
stale one- or two-day-old bread made into crumbs by blending or processing.

BURGHUL also known as bulghur or bulgar wheat; hulled steamed wheat kernels that, once dried, are crushed into various size grains. Not the same as cracked wheat.

BUTTERMILK originally the term given to the slightly sour liquid left after butter was churned from cream, today it is commercially made similarly to yogurt. Sold alongside all fresh milk products in supermarkets; despite the implication of its name, it is low in fat.

CAPSICUM also known as pepper or bell pepper; can be red, green, yellow, orange or purplish-black. Discard seeds and membranes before use.

CHEESE
bocconcini walnut-sized, fresh semi-soft baby mozzarella.
cottage fresh, white, unripened curd cheese with a grainy consistency.
cream commonly known as Philly or Philadelphia, a soft cows-milk cheese.
fetta white cheese with a milky, fresh acidity; commonly made from cows milk, though sheep and goats milk varieties are available.
jarlsberg a Norwegian cheese made from cows' milk; has large holes and a mild, nutty taste.
mozzarella soft, spun-curd cheese; has a low melting point and wonderfully elastic texture when heated.
parmesan also known as parmigiano, a hard, grainy, cows-milk cheese.
pecorino the generic Italian name for cheeses made from sheep milk. It's a hard, white to pale yellow cheese.
pizza a commercial blend of varying proportions of processed grated mozzarella, cheddar and parmesan.
ricotta the name for this soft, grainy, cows-milk cheese roughly translates as cooked again. Made from whey, a by-product of other cheese-making.
romano a hard, sheep or cows-milk cheese. Straw-coloured and grainy in texture; parmesan can be substituted.
swiss generic name for a variety of cheeses originating in Switzerland.

CHICKPEAS also called garbanzos, hummus or channa; an irregularly round, sandy-coloured legume. Available canned or dried (the latter need several hours soaking before use).

CORIANDER also known as pak chee, cilantro or chinese parsley; a bright-green-leafed herb having both pungent aroma and taste. The stems and roots are also used in Thai cooking: wash well before chopping. Also available ground or as seeds. These should not be substituted for fresh coriander as the tastes are completely different.

CORN FLAKE CRUMBS made from crushed corn flakes.

COUSCOUS a fine grain-like cereal product made from semolina.

DRIED CRANBERRIES used in sweet and savoury dishes; has the slightly sour, succulent flavour of fresh cranberries.

ENGLISH MUFFINS round yeast-risen teacakes often confused with crumpets.

FIVE-SPICE POWDER a fragrant mix of ground cinnamon, cloves, star anise, sichuan pepper and fennel seeds. Also known as chinese five-spice.

FLOUR
cornflour also known as cornstarch.
plain an all-purpose flour made from wheat.
self-raising plain flour that has been sifted with baking powder in the proportion of 1 cup flour to 2 teaspoons baking powder.

GELATINE a thickening agent. Available in sheet form, known as leaf gelatine or as a powder. Three teaspoons of dried gelatine (8g or one sachet) is roughly equivalent to four gelatine leaves.

GINGER also known as green or root ginger; the thick root of a tropical plant.

GOLDEN SYRUP a by-product of refined sugarcane; pure maple syrup or honey can be substituted.

HUMMUS a Middle-Eastern dip made from softened dried chickpeas, garlic, lemon juice and tahini (sesame seed paste); can be purchased, ready-made, from most supermarkets.

KIWIFRUIT also known as chinese gooseberry; having a brown, somewhat hairy skin and bright-green flesh with a unique sweet-tart flavour.

KUMARA Polynesian name of orange-fleshed sweet potato often confused with yam.

MESCLUN a salad mix of assorted young lettuce and other green leaves, including baby spinach leaves, mizuna and curly endive.

MUSHROOMS
button small and white with a delicate, subtle flavour. If a recipe calls for an unspecified mushroom, use button.
oyster also known as abalone; grey-white mushroom shaped like a fan. Prized for their smooth texture and subtle, oyster-like flavour.
swiss brown also known as cremini or roman; light to dark-brown mushrooms with full-bodied flavour. Button or cup mushrooms can be substituted.

NOODLES
fresh rice also known as ho fun, sen yau, khao pun, pho or kway tiau, depending on the country of manufacture. Can be purchased in strands of various widths (thin or wide) or as large sheets weighing about 500g, which are then cut into the noodle size desired. Chewy and pure white, they do not need pre-cooking before use.
rice stick also known assen lek, ho fun or kway teow; come in different widths. Soak in hot water to soften.
rice vermicelli also known as sen mee, mei fun or bee hoon; made with rice flour. Soak dried noodles in hot water until softened then boil them briefly and rinse with hot water.

PANCETTA Italian bacon that is cured, but not smoked. Substitute with bacon.

PARSLEY, FLAT-LEAF a flat-leaf variety of parsley also known as continental or italian parsley.

PASTA
farfalle bow-tie shaped short pasta; sometimes known as butterfly pasta.
penne translated literally as 'quills'. A ridged pasta cut into short lengths on the diagonal.
risoni small rice-shape pasta; very similar to another small pasta, orzo.

RICE
koshihikari small, round-grain white rice. If unavailable, substitute a white short-grain rice such as arborio and cook using the absorption method.

rice paper sheets also known as banh trang. Made from rice paste and stamped into rounds, are quite brittle and will break if dropped. Dipped in water they become pliable wrappers for food and uncooked vegetables. Make good spring-roll wrappers.

ROLLED OATS flattened oat grain rolled into flakes; most often used for porridge.

ROLLED RICE flattened rice grain rolled into flakes; looks similar to rolled oats.

ROLLED RYE flattened rye grain rolled into flakes; looks similar to rolled oats.

SAMBAL OELEK (also ulek or olek) a salty paste made from ground chillies and vinegar. Available in Asian food stores and supermarkets.

SAUCES
barbecue a spicy, tomato-based sauce.
char siu a Chinese barbecue sauce made from sugar, water, salt, fermented soybean paste, honey, soy sauce, malt syrup and spices. It can be found at most supermarkets.
cranberry made of cranberries cooked in sugar syrup.
fish also called naam pla or nuoc naam. Made from pulverised salted fermented fish (most often anchovies); has a strong taste and pungent smell, so use sparingly.
hoisin a thick, sweet and spicy Chinese paste made from salted fermented soy beans, onions and garlic.
oyster a thick, richly-flavoured brown sauce made from oysters and their brine, cooked with salt and soy sauce, and thickened with starches.
soy also known as sieu; is made from fermented soy beans. Several variations are available; we use a mild Japanese variety in our recipes.
Japanese soy is an all-purpose low-sodium sauce made with more wheat content than its Chinese counterparts. *Light soy* is a fairly thin, pale and salty sauce. Not to be confused with salt-reduced or low-sodium soy sauces.
sweet chilli a mild sauce made from red chillies, sugar, garlic and vinegar.
teriyaki a Japanese sauce; made from soy sauce, mirin, sugar, ginger and other spices.

SAVOIARDI SPONGE FINGER BISCUITS also known as Savoy biscuits, lady's fingers or sponge fingers; they are long, oval-shaped, Italian-style crisp fingers made from sponge-cake mixture.

SPINACH also known as english spinach and, incorrectly, silver beet.

STAR ANISE a dried star-shaped fruit having an astringent aniseed or licorice flavour.

STARFRUIT also known as carambola, five-corner fruit or chinese star fruit; pale green or yellow colour. Has a clean, crisp texture, and the flavour may be either sweet or sour, depending on the variety and when picked. Doesn't need to be peeled or seeded.

SULTANAS dried grapes, also known as golden raisins.

SUMAC a purple-red, astringent spice ground from berries growing on shrubs that flourish wild around the Mediterranean; adds a tart, lemony flavour to dips and meats.

TAHINI sesame-seed paste available from health-food stores.

VANILLA
bean dried long, thin pod from a tropical golden orchid; the minuscule black seeds inside the bean imparts a luscious vanilla flavour in baking and desserts.
extract obtained from vanilla beans infused in alcohol and water.

VINEGAR
balsamic made from the juice of Trebbiano grapes; it is a deep rich brown with a sweet and sour flavour.
red wine based on fermented red wine.
rice a colourless vinegar made from fermented rice and flavoured with sugar and salt. Also known as seasoned rice vinegar.
white made from spirit of cane sugar.
white wine made from white wine.

WOMBOK also known as peking cabbage, chinese cabbage or petsai. Elongated in shape with pale green, crinkly leaves, this is the most common cabbage in South-East Asian cooking.

ZUCCHINI also known as courgette.

Conversion chart

MEASURES

One Australian metric measuring cup holds approximately 250ml; one Australian metric tablespoon holds 20ml; one Australian metric teaspoon holds 5ml.

The difference between one country's measuring cups and another's is within a two- or three-teaspoon variance, and will not affect your cooking results. North America, New Zealand and the United Kingdom use a 15ml tablespoon.

All cup and spoon measurements are level. The most accurate way of measuring dry ingredients is to weigh them. When measuring liquids, use a clear glass or plastic jug with the metric markings.

We use large eggs with an average weight of 60g.

DRY MEASURES

METRIC	IMPERIAL
15g	½oz
30g	1oz
60g	2oz
90g	3oz
125g	4oz (¼lb)
155g	5oz
185g	6oz
220g	7oz
250g	8oz (½lb)
280g	9oz
315g	10oz
345g	11oz
375g	12oz (¾lb)
410g	13oz
440g	14oz
470g	15oz
500g	16oz (1lb)
750g	24oz (1½lb)
1kg	32oz (2lb)

LIQUID MEASURES

METRIC	IMPERIAL
30ml	1 fluid oz
60ml	2 fluid oz
100ml	3 fluid oz
125ml	4 fluid oz
150ml	5 fluid oz (¼ pint/1 gill)
190ml	6 fluid oz
250ml	8 fluid oz
300ml	10 fluid oz (½ pint)
500ml	16 fluid oz
600ml	20 fluid oz (1 pint)
1000ml (1 litre)	1¾ pints

LENGTH MEASURES

METRIC	IMPERIAL
3mm	⅛in
6mm	¼in
1cm	½in
2cm	¾in
2.5cm	1in
5cm	2in
6cm	2½in
8cm	3in
10cm	4in
13cm	5in
15cm	6in
18cm	7in
20cm	8in
23cm	9in
25cm	10in
28cm	11in
30cm	12in (1ft)

OVEN TEMPERATURES

These oven temperatures are only a guide for conventional ovens. For fan-forced ovens, check the manufacturer's manual.

	°C (CELSIUS)	°F (FAHRENHEIT)	GAS MARK
Very slow	120	250	½
Slow	150	275-300	1-2
Moderately slow	160	325	3
Moderate	180	350-375	4-5
Moderately hot	200	400	6
Hot	220	425-450	7-8
Very hot	240	475	9

Index

General manager *Christine Whiston*
Editorial director *Susan Tomnay*
Creative director & designer *Hieu Chi Nguyen*
Senior editor *Wendy Bryant*
Food director *Pamela Clark*
Food editor *Louise Patniotis*
Nutritional information *Belinda Farlow*
Special feature photographer *Tanya Zouev*
Special feature stylist *Sarah DeNardi*
Special feature food preparation *Belinda Farlow*

Director of sales *Brian Cearnes*
Marketing manager *Bridget Cody*
Business analyst *Ashley Davies*
Operations manager *David Scotto*
International rights enquiries *Laura Bamford*
lbamford@acpuk.com

acp books

ACP Books are published by ACP Magazines
a division of PBL Media Pty Limited
Group publisher, Women's lifestyle *Pat Ingram*
Director of sales, Women's lifestyle *Lynette Phillips*
Commercial manager, Women's lifestyle *Seymour Cohen*
Marketing director, Women's lifestyle *Matthew Dominello*
Public relations manager, Women's lifestyle *Hannah Deveraux*
Creative director, Events, Women's lifestyle *Luke Bonnano*
Research Director, Women's lifestyle *Justin Stone*
ACP Magazines, Chief Executive officer *Scott Lorson*
PBL Media, Chief Executive officer *Ian Law*

Cover *Corn, cheese and carrot omelettes p18*
Cover photographer *Joshua Dasey*
Cover stylist *Justine Osborne*

Photographers *Andre Martin, Andrew Young, Brett Stevens, Ian Wallace, Joshua Dasey, Prue Ruscoe, Rob Palmer, Steve Brown, Tanya Zouev*
Stylists *Wendy Berecry, Julz Beresford, Kate Brown, Marie-Helene Clauzon, Michaela le Compte, Trish Heagerty, David Morgan, Sarah O'Brien, Justine Osborne*

Produced by ACP Books, Sydney.
Published by ACP Books, a division of ACP Magazines Ltd.
54 Park St, Sydney NSW Australia 2000. GPO Box 4088, Sydney, NSW 2001.
Phone +61 2 9282 8618 Fax +61 2 9267 9438
acpbooks@acpmagazines.com.au www.acpbooks.com.au
Printed by SNP Leefung, Hong Kong.
Australia Distributed by Network Services, GPO Box 4088, Sydney, NSW 2001.
Phone +61 2 9282 8777 Fax +61 2 9264 3278
networkweb@networkservicescompany.com.au
United Kingdom Distributed by Australian Consolidated Press (UK),
10 Scirocco Close, Moulton Park Office Village, Northampton, NN3 6AP.
Phone +44 1604 642 200 Fax +44 1604 642 300
books@acpuk.com www.acpuk.com
New Zealand Distributed by Netlink Distribution Company, ACP Media Centre,
Cnr Fanshawe and Beaumont Streets, Westhaven, Auckland.
PO Box 47906, Ponsonby, Auckland, NZ.
Phone +64 9 366 9966 Fax 0800 277 412 ask@ndc.co.nz
South Africa Distributed by PSD Promotions, 30 Diesel Road Isando, Gauteng
Johannesburg. PO Box 1175, Isando 1600, Gauteng Johannesburg.
Phone +27 11 392 6065/6/7 Fax +27 11 392 6079/80 orders@psdprom.co.za
Canada Distributed by Publishers Group Canada
Order Desk & Customer Service 9050 Shaughnessy Street, Vancouver, BC V6P 6E5
Phone (800) 663 5714 Fax (800) 565 3770 service@raincoast.com

Kids' Cooking for Health: the Australian women's weekly
Includes index.
ISBN 978 1 86396 757 0 (pbk.).
1. Cookery (Natural foods). 2. Children – Nutrition.
I.Clark, Pamela. II. Title: Australian women's weekly.
641.5622
© ACP Magazines Ltd 2008
ABN 18 053 273 546

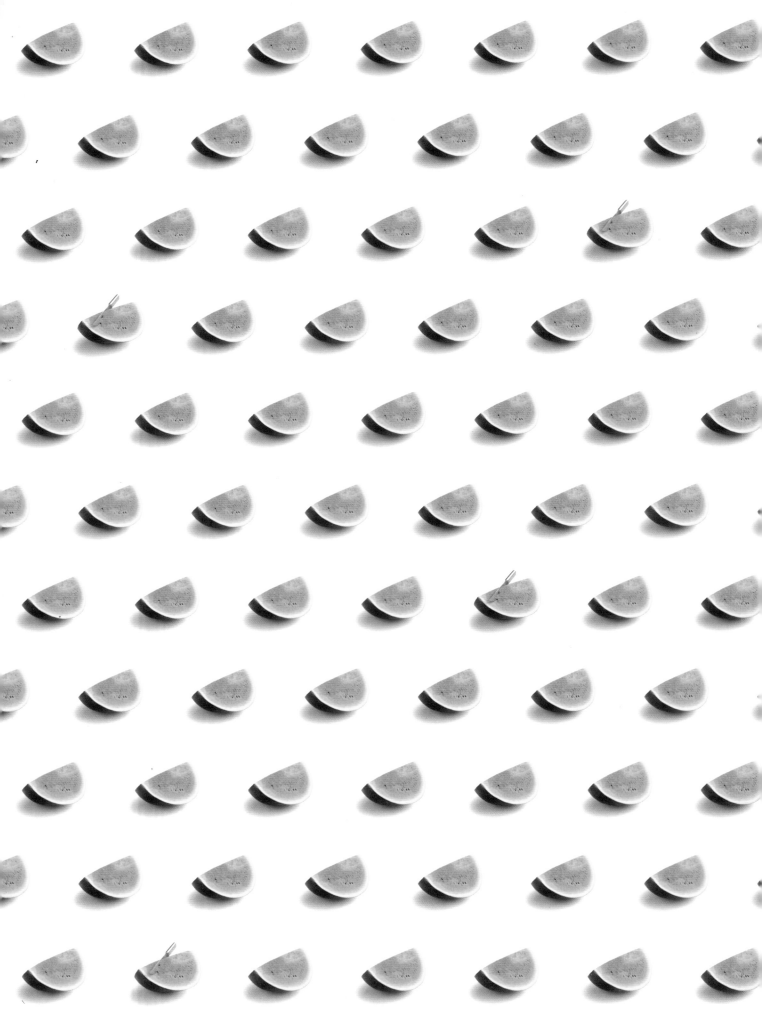